For Mary

WHOSE VOICE I LIKE

LUCIFER IN HARNESS

American Meter, Metaphor, and Diction

Edwin Fussell

PRINCETON UNIVERSITY PRESS

Library of Congress Catalog Card Number: 72-4040

International Standard Book Number: 0-691-06238-2

This book has been composed in Linotype Times Roman

Printed in the United States of America
by Princeton University Press

LUCIFER IN HARNESS

Late in the afternoon the mocking-bird, the American mimic,
 singing in the Great Dismal Swamp

WHITMAN, "Our Old Feuillage"

Contents

Preface

MY TITLE comes from an early poem by Robert Lowell ("Between the Porch and the Altar" in *Lord Weary's Castle*) and the passage in which the phrase occurs reads as follows:

> Here the Lord
> Is Lucifer in harness: hand on sword,
> He watches me for Mother, and will turn
> The bier and baby-carriage where I burn.

The multiple applications of the title should duly emerge. Lest they proliferate too wildly, or, worse, fail to emerge at all, let me offer a few loose guidelines. (Guidelines to titles ought to be loose. As Whitman was forever saying, the reader has his work to do too.) Loosely speaking, then, Lucifer is the frustrated and rebellious American poet in harness to the English language and English literary tradition. Mother (Super-Mom) is England. The bier and baby-carriage images, fused, signify death-birth, that is, historical process. It will hardly be contested that the American poets have in this situation for nearly two centuries been doing a slow burn.

This is not a literary history, although it implies one, but a triptych of essays, attempts to explore the fundamental dilemma of American poetry as it appears in the three crucial fields of meter, metaphor, and poetic diction, the three crucial fields of American poetry (taken as a whole) most studiously avoided by American scholars, but not, as I intend to show, by American poets. The book is short, by design. Essays are not supposed to be overkill. I was after theory.

Any poetic theory depends on the choice of poets. My premise is that a theory of American poetry can stand only as it begins to accommodate Poe and Whitman, and then connects them in traditional continuity with Pound, Eliot, and Williams. The next most important poets—not absolutely essential to the argument but eminently useful for the side lights they throw on it—are Hart Crane and Wallace Stevens. Emerson is of considerable value for the stimulus of his ideas; much less so for his poetry. The "bad" poets, most notably Bryant and James Russell Lowell, are indispensable as evidence of how and why American poetry can sometimes go so wrong. Emily Dickinson—decidedly a special case; most of her work is unfinished, so that there is no final text to rely on—Edwin Arlington Robinson, and Robert Frost I allude to from time to time. Clearly they are not "bad" poets, even by avant-garde standards; neither are they at the center of the oyster.

That is the batting order. Readers who anticipate a different batting order may suffer pangs of disappointment. Naturally, I hope to bring them around a little to my point of view; if not, they can always suffer the thrills of outrage. I still contend that the poets here emphasized are quite enough to keep anybody's head spinning for a good long time, especially in view of the fact that they are commonly regarded as unrelated or antithetical. If there is one thing clear in this great dismal swamp it is that the reader of Whitman is not likely to be a reader of Pound, and vice versa.

I have called this book a triptych of essays. That is its external form. Its internal form is a progression of styles. The first essay is mainly expository and as lucid as I could make it, hoping thereby to open the subject with the least possible confusion. The second essay, which is much the most difficult in its theory, is necessarily more closely analytical. At the same time, it is also, stylistically, more relaxed, allusive, freewheeling, and intermittently passionate (doubtless because of the intrusion of the Civil War); I have done my best to keep these potentially anarchic qualities under strict control. The third chapter is the least conventional of the three. I assume that by then the reader will have the argument thoroughly in hand and will be prepared to relax his customary expectations about what literary criticism is and go along with a somewhat more imaginative approach. If I have offended the common sense or good taste of the well-disposed reader, I am genuinely sorry. If I have made even a slight dent in the bulwarks of the American literary establishment, I am delighted.

My subject is the great American poets. Style should follow subject. I have tried to write as much like my poets as I could get away with—always bearing in mind the necessity of being clear to the reader. But being clear to the reader does not mean being *immediately* clear to the reader (he may, from time to time, have to pause for reflection), nor does it mean that *everything* has to be explained. There are in this book no conventional *explications de texte*. I am weary of them, and I suspect that most readers share my feeling. Readers have minds of their own. Given the general principles and facts, and a handful of carefully selected examples, they can very well follow the ball game themselves and get a lot more fun out of it. And if criticism isn't fun for the reader, it had better not be written.

Thanks are in order to Donald Wesling, who read the entire manuscript and gave help when I most needed it; to Edward R. Weismiller, Roy Harvey Pearce, and my brother, Paul Fussell, Jr., who helped with the first essay; to R. Miriam Brokaw and other editors at the Princeton University Press, who read the manuscript in an early stage and offered tough and sympathetic advice; to Carol Orr, who took it from there to the end, miraculously managing to handle the book with tender loving care, while (thank God!) making no compromises with the highest professional standards; and to my wife, Mary Burton Fussell, whose support and assistance have been so extensive and unremitting that I sometimes think she has the entire book by heart.

An earlier version of the essay entitled "The Meter-Making Argument" was originally published in *Aspects of American Poetry*, edited by Richard M. Ludwig, copyright © 1962 by the Ohio University Press. It is reprinted here with the gracious consent of Weldon A. Kefauver, Director of the Ohio State University Press, and of the original editor. A brief excerpt from "What the Thunder Said" appeared in the *Virginia Woolf Quarterly* (Summer 1973), through the generous hospitality of the editor, Suzanne Henig.

Finally, I must thank the following publishers and people for permission to quote material in copyright or in which they have human rights:

Beacon Press, for William Carlos Williams, *I Wanted to Write a Poem*, © 1958 by William Carlos Williams.

Jonathan Cape Ltd, and the Estate of Robert Frost, for British rights to *The Poetry of Robert Frost*, ed. Edward Connery Lathem (for copyright dates, see Holt, Rinehart and Winston).

Chandler Publishing Company, for their facsimile edition of the 1855 edition of *Leaves of Grass*.

Doubleday & Company, Inc., for *Selected Poems of Herman Melville*, ed. Hennig Cohen, and copyright © 1964 by Hennig Cohen.

Faber and Faber Ltd, for British rights to John Berryman, *The Dream Songs* (for copyright dates, see Farrar, Straus & Giroux); T. S. Eliot, *Collected Poems, 1909-1962* (for copyright dates, see Harcourt Brace Jovanovich); Wallace Stevens, *Collected Poems* (for copyright dates, see Random House-Alfred A. Knopf).

Farrar, Straus & Giroux, Inc., for John Berryman, *The Dream Songs*, copyright © 1959, 1962, 1963, 1964, 1965, 1966, 1967, 1968, 1969 by John Berryman.

Harcourt Brace Jovanovich, Inc., for T. S. Eliot, *Collected Poems, 1909-1962*, copyright © 1962, 1963 by Thomas Stearns Eliot (the mysteriously unidentified sentence on p. 131, below, is of course the final line of "The Love Song of J. Alfred Prufrock"); and for Robert Lowell, *Lord Weary's Castle*, copyright 1944, 1946 by Robert Lowell.

Harvard University Press (The Belknap Press), for vol. I (*Poems*) of *Collected Works of Edgar Allan Poe*, ed. Thomas Ollive Mabbott, copyright © 1969 by the President and Fellows of Harvard College.

Holt, Rinehart and Winston, Inc., for excerpts from "The Oven Bird" and "After Apple-Picking," from *The Poetry of Robert Frost*, ed. Edward Connery Lathem, copyright 1916, 1930, 1939, © 1969 by Holt, Rinehart and Winston, Inc.; copyright 1944, © 1958 by Robert Frost; copyright © 1967 by Lesley Frost Ballantine. Reprinted by permission of Holt, Rinehart and Winston, Inc.

Liveright, for *The Collected Poems and Selected Letters and Prose of Hart Crane*, copyright © 1933, 1958, 1966 by Liveright Publishing Corporation.

All else is "fair use." Unless there was some good reason to quote from a first edition, or a facsimile edition, I have quoted from the latest definitive texts. This already swollen list of names and dates need not be extended by adding them. The well-read critic knows what they are, and the common reader couldn't care less. I especially want to thank Robert Lowell for letting me lift my title from his poem; without it, I should be badly off. I also want to thank John Crowe Ransom for permission to quote from "Philomela"; without it, the book might never have started. Unfortunately, all my other poets are dead.

Chapter One

THE METER-MAKING ARGUMENT

Dissonance and Dialectic

Ah, but our numbers are not felicitous,
It goes not liquidly for us.

RANSOM, "Philomela"

INDEED it does not. At first by default, later by design, American numbers are recurrently characterized by that "dissonance" with which John Crowe Ransom charges himself personally in this delightful poem, and of which he professes (such is the casuistry of poets) to be "sick." The lines containing these mock complaints are by the most cunning artistry metrically harsh. With obvious ironic relish, the poem also insists upon jarring our ears with such studied cacophonies as "pernoctated," such unnecessary inversions as "To England came Philomela with her pain." By diligent avoidance of liquidity, "Philomela" achieves an undeniable and unmistakable American rightness.

The poem tells first of the wanderings of Philomela ("lover of song," the spirit of poetry) from Greece to Rome, thence to the continent, and finally to England, but not to America:

Philomela, Philomela, lover of song,
I am in despair if we may make us worthy,
A bantering breed sophistical and swarthy;
Unto more beautiful, persistently more young,
Thy fabulous provinces belong.

(Patent irony. Who else besides the Americans are sophistical and swarthy? And what in this context can "persistently more young" mean but persistently more naive?) In one country after another she utters herself "in the classic numbers of the nightingale." But

3

"classic" can hardly refer with equal propriety to the numbers of such various poetic traditions, and in fact Ransom himself seems dubious about both the French and German. Moreover, as Ransom well knows, the nightingale is to the American imagination the arch symbol, both lusted after and hated, of the English tradition, whose liquidity he professes to desire while in the act of demolishing it.[1]

More specifically the poem tells of Ransom as a student at Oxford hearing "from the darkest wood" the "fairy numbers" of the nightingale. (The tone recalls Keats, but "Philomela" is more significantly an Americanized version of Arnold's poem by the same name.) To his "capacious" ear—a pun in praise of the Americans' willingness to entertain a wider variety of musical delight than the British—"Her classics registered a little flat!/ I rose, and venomously spat." It is then that Ransom deviously declares his doubt if we may make us worthy. But the poem itself works the other way; it is eminently worthy, and entirely on its own terms, which are pointedly and persistently antagonistic to the British tradition. What "Philomela" tells us, finally, is that subject matter is of small importance to the national quality of a poetry (the poet shows no interest in the bird except as she sings), but that technique, and especially metric, is of the essence. "Philomela" tells us also, and shows us, that the American poet is indeed "inordinate" but can turn to account what he may not in any case avoid, a literary situation dominated by deprivation and therefore by excessive national self-consciousness and resentment, manageable only by desperate remedies born of frustration and tension.

---

[1] Cf. Wallace Stevens in "Autumn Refrain":

> The yellow moon of words about the nightingale
> In measureless measures, not a bird for me
> But the name of a bird and the name of a nameless air
> I have never—shall never hear.

Modern American poetry is full of such jokes, which are pitfalls for the unwary. William Carlos Williams' *Paterson* opens with an invocation describing the poem as "a reply to Greek and Latin with the bare hands." Well and good, if "reply" means emulation of a lost music which must now be re-created on wholly new terms. But if "reply" means "retort," and it sounds as if it does, then we have only another trap for the innocent. How could it possibly be the ancients, with their dead languages, against whom the American poet must contend, except perhaps in a kind of harmless but revealing fantasy? For "Greek and Latin" read "British." "Bare hands" are the hard actualities of American life, the hardest of which, but also the most exhilarating, is the nearly impossible situation in which the American poet finds himself. Book One of *Paterson* ends with a quotation from John Addington Symonds' *Studies of the Greek Poets*, dealing with the relations between metrical wrenching and distorted subjects, "as well as their agreement with the snarling spirit of the satirist." Once more, felicity resides in dislocation, or, alternatively, in looseness, for perhaps no important American poem (Pound's *Cantos* possibly excepted) is so variously chaotic in its meters.

Deliberately, of course. As Williams remarks later on in *Paterson:*

> Dissonance
> (if you are interested)
> leads to discovery

All this dissonance and looseness ought to be very appealing to the reader of American poetry; it goes not so liquidly for us either. Perhaps we can take a little comfort from the perplexities of the people who were actually on the scene. In "Notes from Conversations with George W. Whitman, 1893: Mostly in his own Words,"

5

Horace L. Traubel recorded for us the following indispensable vignette: "I remember mother comparing Hiawatha to Walt's, and the one seemed to us pretty much the same muddle as the other. Mother said that if Hiawatha was poetry, perhaps Walt's was." Mother and George may have been a little muddled, but not much more so than we historians of American poetry. Whenever we think of it as a simple separate subject, we find ourselves as balked and bewildered as the American poets whose story we try to tell. And in truth we are not much more enterprising than the Whitman family: faced with such queerly assorted poets as Longfellow and Whitman, Poe and Pound, Stevens and Eliot, we either incline to pretend that some of these poets are "in the American tradition" (undefined), while others are not, or we panic, and declare the whole problem insoluble, saying, in effect, "There is no such thing as American poetry." What if instead we simply accept the dissonance and dialectic of American poetry and try to account for them? With these as starting points, a theory of American poetry immediately begins to take shape, and precisely from those paradoxical pairs of poets who otherwise most baffle our formulations. Naturally, the poets and the issues will never line up perfectly; still, the diverse, or even antithetical kinds of poems we associate with their names sufficiently suggest the fundamental divisions underlying the superficial confusion in American poetry.

Some American poets are intensely nationalistic in their attitudes toward poetry, while others are scarcely national. Some American poets are in open revolt against what they conceive to be the English tradition, while others are perhaps too comfortable in it. Thus Anglophile Melville (in "Dupont's Round Fight"):

> In time and measure perfect moves
>   All Art whose aim is sure;
> Evolving rhyme and stars divine
>   Have rules, and they endure.

Wrong from the start. Against Melville set William Carlos Williams, who, of all the important American poets, had as a father a British citizen: "To the English, English is England: 'History is England,' yodels Mr. Eliot. To us this is not so, not so *if* we prove it by writing a poem built to refute it" ("The Poem as a Field of Action").[2] As Wallace Stevens says, "Nothing could be more inappropriate to American literature than its English source since the Americans are not British in sensibility" ("Adagia"). Even though that statement requires considerable amplification and some modification, it is persuasive enough on the main point: no treatment of American poetry can offer much unless it concentrates on the conflict between the aspirations of the nationalistic American poet and the all but overwhelming authority of the English tradition.

My own inclination is to press toward an understanding of that conflict by trying to talk about American poetry technically and culturally (especially with respect to politics) at the same time. For tutelary spirit I invoke Emerson, and most of all seize upon his talismanic phrase about a "meter-making argument." For on closer inspection, and imaginatively understood, that phrase turns out to be nationalistic as well as metrical. Granted, it makes very little difference whether we start with meter, metaphor, or diction: the issues are the same in all three. Still, there is a kind of priority about meter, even without Emerson's say-so. First, meter is that element of poetic technique through which the American poet has directed the greater part of his poetical energy, especially when self-consciously engendering a native tradition, and it is therefore the metric of American poetry that most obviously differs from (while at the same time it most clearly relates to) English poetry.

---

[2] "When I was inclined to write poems, I was very definitely an American kid, confident of himself and also independent. From the beginning I felt I was *not* English" (*I Wanted to Write a Poem*). This late statement hardly jibes with Williams' early struggle to escape the influence of Keats.

7

Second, meter is easier to discuss than more elusive qualities like metaphor and diction.

And of course, there is a much more important reason. Although prosodic descriptions, just because they are radically simplified, are predictably crude, the poetic qualities they point to, rhythm and motion, are anything but crude. These are the soul of the poem, which comes into being only as language moves in discernible and cumulative patterns of recurrence and progress, from first word to last, through action to substance. The poem itself is how the language moves and where it arrives. Ideally, the poem arrives at a finality of statement (different for every poem) wherein it is impossible to distinguish whether our satisfaction derives from its truth, or its beauty, or its goodness. Of these metaphysical properties, meter is the first occasion and investiture. And if this is so of one poem, then it is so of all poems, or of any group of poems selected on reasonably homogeneous principles. Therefore we can say that the soul of American poetry dwells in its rhythm, and that we can approach that soul, however imperfectly, through metrical analysis.

So much for technique and transcendentals. If we approach American poetry from the opposite direction—from the national rather than the poetic side—we come to the same conclusion. Quite in addition to the fact that meters are always of the essence, American meters are strikingly and peculiarly symptomatic of the long-standing ambivalence in cultural (or political) relations between America and Great Britain. Indeed, it is not too much to say that American meters shift with the shifting harmonic overtones of the cultural relations between the two countries, or even, conversely, that a metrical shift on one side of the water may have political consequences on the other side, as in the latter nineteenth century *Leaves of Grass* by its rhythms as much as its message induced in the British intellectual and workingman alike a kindlier and more respectful attitude toward the upstart States. Not that such communication was or is perfect. Conservatism is after all conservatism and the penny-a-line mind is the same on Grub Street and on Madison Avenue. In the Appendix to the 1856 edition of *Leaves of Grass*, Whitman gleefully quoted such British inanities as these: "We do not, then, fear this Walt Whitman, who gives us slang in the place of melody, and rowdyism in the place of regularity. The depth of his indecencies will be the grave of his fame." At least as early as the American Revolution, the British have had a bad record for sensing the shape of things to come. Another penny-a-liner quoted by Whitman remarked that "the external form, therefore, is startling, and by no means seductive, to English ears, accustomed to the sumptuous music of ordinary metre."

No matter how willfully idiosyncratic the poet, nor how unconscious his involvement, the poems he makes are not monads, but members of a poetry, and poetries are for the most part distinctively national. Any of them—let us say the English—lies within a tradition of shared sensibility and culture, expressed in a particular language, with a national bias derived from the deeply-felt identity of a people. Ordinarily somewhat diffuse, this deeply-felt sense of community is sharpened and articulated and stabilized by poets, with the consequence that in an actual national poetry, technique, sensibility, and culture are absolutely inextricable one from another, each being the intensified instrument and expression of the others.

But that description holds only when language and nation coincide, as in American poetry they assuredly do not. The American poet is a non-Englishman (frequently an anti-Englishman) writing in the English language. And always complaining. "We poets have to talk in a language which is not English," complains Williams (in *Paterson*), who is always talking on the subject, "It is the American idiom." That statement is about half true. True, there is an American vernacular or idiom, and the best American poets stick close to it. False, we do not speak the English language. We do. The American vernacular is not a separate language, but a sub-species

9

of the English language that we share with the British, Canadians, Australians, and others. And the divergences are much less significant, statistically speaking, than the identities. But let our most Americanized poet go on talking:

> I always said to myself that I did not speak English, for one thing, and that that should be the basis for a beginning, that I spoke a language that was my own and that I would govern it according to my necessities and not according to unrelated traditions the necessity for whose being had long since passed away. English is full of such compunctions which are wholly irrelevant for a man living as I am today but custom makes it profitable for us to be bound by them. Not me. ("The Basis of Faith in Art")

If Williams were correct in his assertion that he did not in fact speak English, there would be no problem, whereas for Williams there is nothing but problem. As the foregoing passage makes sufficiently clear, it is not really the English language *per se* that is troubling Williams but the sensibility and literature of it.

The American poet's feeling toward the common tongue must always be ambivalent and not infrequently confused. His poetic medium, with all its attendant implications for sensibility and culture, is at once a siren and an albatross. He cannot write in the American vernacular without taking into account the relation of the American vernacular to the English language, and that is both his horror and his opportunity. Always he writes toward and away from the establishment, and the establishment is no simple "foreign domination" but his own linguistic situation. After all, it is his acute sensitivity to the stress and shape and sound of his own culture that leads him to be a poet in the first place, but the stress and shape and sound of his own culture are largely caused by the English language. That he can never escape. Of course, anti-British propaganda is more rampant in our early history. But if the anti-British, pro-American talk and animus died down after Whitman, the literary situation that initially caused them continues in a disguised form and will continue for the foreseeable future. No matter if English culture and English metric no longer directly threaten the American poet; the conservative, metrically regular tradition of England, at first both inescapable and unassimilable, has at length been introjected into the American poetic psyche in an almost Oedipal way (as we might have expected from the original parent-child relation of England and her New World colonies). Children must revolt against their parents; adolescents may, if they choose, revolt against themselves. So doing, they continue to move toward maturity.

Our poetic history begins with the necessary emancipation from English tradition, conceived as inherited but not quite wanted order and regularity. The American poet had to liberate himself from an alien culture and sensibility; ultimately, he had to use the very language of that culture and sensibility to liberate his art from an alien technique and make it his own. Doubtless his problem was exacerbated by the fact that the catchword of the youthful culture was "liberty" and the catchword of the parent culture "order." Unfortunately for the English-speaking American poet, English "order" is nowhere more attractively enshrined than in English poetry; and nowhere is the English poetic tradition more like a red flag to a bullheaded American poet than in its numbers. It is easy for the American citizen to scoff at such eccentricities as the House of Lords, but it is not quite so easy for the American poet to scoff at Shakespeare, Milton, Pope, Wordsworth, *et al.* Their meters must be summarily disposed of (after which we can come back to them). Given the nature of poetry in English, and the facts of American history, free verse is as inevitable as the Declaration of Independence.

There is simply no use arguing, against the general sense of our

11

poets in this matter, that the English tradition comprises a world of variety, or even calling attention to the existence of its several poetic periods and their metrical differences from one another. The poet is not a historical prosodist, but a man whose ear must instruct him how to bring into being meters possible and appropriate to his actual situation. To the ear that has once been attuned to the obviously American cadences of Whitman, the metrical differences among Spenser, Dryden, and Coleridge no longer sound startling. Compared with Whitman, they are all regular, and their regularity consists in a general commitment to the traditionally English syllable-stress metric, to a line most often made up of dissyllabic feet and measured out in pentameter length. To the American ear this regularity tends to sound all of a piece. It smacks of the foreign and the old, sometimes even in American poems otherwise conspicuous for native and modern content: Robinson and Frost are the perfect cases in point. Yet English regularity, before or after introjection, is *the* tradition with which the individual American talent must come to terms, even if the terms are total defiance and rejection. In his *Fable for Critics*, Lowell called the English pentameter—the word "English" being ambiguous—a "sham meter." Nearly a century later, in "The Constant Symbol," Robert Frost compliments himself on having written his verse "regular all this time without knowing till yesterday that it was from fascination with this constant symbol I celebrate." In Frost's view, the "constant symbol" seems to mean the discipline of form. But perhaps this constant symbol of his reveals more than he knows; at any rate, like Lowell's jibe, it points to the American conviction of English regularity.

Ironically, the best evidence that the English tradition seems all of a piece comes from the American poet-critic most comfortable in it. In "Poets and Poetry of the English Language" (1876 version), the essay introducing his anthology *A Library of Poetry and Song*, Bryant not only tells us that "our poetry" is synonymous with "English verse," but also that English prosody became "fixed" between Chaucer and Sidney, and that *The Faerie Queene* represents the English language ("so far as the purposes of poetry require") in a state of "perfection" not subsequently improved upon. So far as Bryant is concerned, the English tradition is *one* tradition, and that tradition is *ours*. Nearly all the American poets agree with him on the first point, I suspect, but few or none on the second. Clearly, Bryant's popular anthology was designed as a respectable repository for more or less uniform gems going "as far back as to the author who may properly be called the father of English poetry," Chaucer, and in the tradition thus asserted, the American poet was expected to find his place. Bryant, Longfellow, Lowell, Holmes, Whittier, and even renegade Emerson found generous places; Poe and N. P. Willis found smaller places; Whitman found no place at all.[3] Given the inherent problem of American poetry, Bryant's perpetual insistence on "models" (as early as 1826, as late as 1876) could have no other issue than an enforced and debilitating conformity with British tradition and especially with British metric. "At the present day [1826] . . . a writer of poems [whether English or American] writes in a language [English] which preceding [English] poets have polished, refined, and filled with forcible, graceful, and musical expressions. He is not only taught by them to overcome the difficulties of rhythmical construction, but he is shown, as it were, the secrets of the mechanism by which he moves the mind of his reader."

So insensitive and uncomprehending a statement, coupled with the rejection of Whitman's poems, immediately strikes us as an ominous sign how close American poetry came to being stillborn. But further reflection, along the lines of the theory of American

[3] I am speaking of the selection of poems in the first edition, 1871. For the second edition, five years later, Bryant excerpted passages from "Out of the Cradle Endlessly Rocking," hopelessly mangling the poem, retitled them "The Mocking-Bird," and placed this new creation among thirty-five other poems about birds, including "To a Waterfowl."

poetry I have been trying to intimate, brings us home to an old and obvious truth: without a Bryant, a Whitman is unimaginable. Moreover, as we shall see, a Whitman conversely makes possible the existence of later and much more complex Bryants. American poetry emerges from dialectic tension, and dialectic requires two opposing terms. Which is not to say that the Bryants have 20-20 vision or are in any respect the equal of the Whitmans.

The Radical Tradition in American Poetry

> There are always two parties, the party of the Past and the
> party of the Future; the Establishment and the Movement.
>
> EMERSON, "Historic Notes of Life and Letters in New England"

AMERICAN POETRY curiously resembles the two-party system
of American politics, where one party invents (sometimes over-
stepping the bounds of possibility, sometimes only pretending to
invent) and the other party alternatively obstructs and then con-
solidates and tries to take credit for the innovations it obstructed.
Both parties have been around long enough to have proved they
are necessary, and perhaps a kind of achievement is possible for
either, but in poetry as in politics the driving force behind historical
development is nearly always found in the party of the Future, or
in Emerson's ever-ready phrase, the Movement. Cultural change
originates with the sensibility that is disturbed by the world it in-
herits and consequently avails itself of the intelligence and courage
to change it. A theory of American poetry can only begin with the
isolation and definition of the radical tradition in poetic technique.

Fortunately, this radical tradition is easily identified; and ascrip-
tion to it of primary historical importance accords with the most
scrupulous critical standards. The radical tradition immediately
disengages itself from the welter of American poetry as soon as we
ask the question of questions: Who are the major and crucial
American poets, both in literary excellence and in the difference
they made to their successors? Two American poets preeminently
answer this description: Whitman and Pound. The other nineteenth-
century poets pass between Whitman's legs like Lilliputians. Possi-
bly he was endowed with that much more poetic talent than the
rest, but how can we tell except as the talent proves itself in action?

The most persuasive proof of Whitman's genius is the perspicacity with which he sensed the poetic needs of his time and place and the almost flawless rectitude with which, in his theory and in his finest poems, he rose to meet them. As he said in his 1855 preface, "A heroic person walks at his ease through and out of that custom or precedent or authority that suits him not. . . . Nothing is finer than silent defiance advancing from new free forms. . . . The cleanest expression is that which finds no sphere worthy of itself and makes one." (The description is equally valid for Pound, except that Pound had a model.) In "Walt Whitman and His Poems" (c. 1855-56), Whitman spoke of "the new versification," and made quite clear that "the old usages of poets afford Walt Whitman no means sufficiently fit and free, and he rejects the old usages." Indeed, so much was sufficiently evident on the first page of the 1855 *Leaves of Grass*, where the opening lines not only promulge the new versification but discuss it in terms of a contrast between perfumes and fresh air:

> I celebrate myself,
> And what I assume you shall assume,
> For every atom belonging to me as good belongs to you.

> I loafe and invite my soul,
> I lean and loafe at my ease . . . . observing a spear
>   of summer grass.

> Houses and rooms are full of perfumes . . . . the shelves are
>   crowded with perfumes,
> I breathe the fragrance myself, and know it and like it,
> The distillation would intoxicate me also,
>   but I shall not let it.

16

The atmosphere is not a perfume . . . . it has no taste of the
      distillation . . . . it is odorless,
It is for my mouth forever . . . . I am in love with it,
I will go to the bank by the wood and become
      undisguised and naked,
I am mad for it to be in contact with me.

Some of this can be analyzed by conventional English scansion. The first triplet, for example, is basically iambic, with lines of three, then four, and then (the sum of three and four) seven feet. Later the verse turns trochaic ("Houses and rooms are full of perfumes"; the line incidentally contains a cunningly concealed internal rhyme. There is another nice one on "be" and "me" in the final line). But everyone feels that scansion of Whitman somehow misses the point. As Whitman said in "Notes Left Over," "The truest and greatest *Poetry*, (while subtly and necessarily always rhythmic, and distinguishable easily enough,) can never again, in the English language, be express'd in arbitrary and rhyming metre." Needless to say, Whitman has many other rhythmic styles, though this one is fairly representative of them all. Needless to add, Whitman is not as many light years away from the English tradition as he would like us to believe. The point is that Whitman is at last free, free to dispose his stresses, his sound patterns, his line lengths, as they please his own ear, and not according to the demands of some prescriptive prosody.

By common agreement, even among those who cannot—because they will not—read his verses, and therefore fancy a distaste for them, Pound is the chief instigator of twentieth-century poetry in English. (But Pound does not call it "English": his term for the basic text of the *Cantos* is "American.") T. S. Eliot has been telling us for years of his own dependence upon Pound (*il miglior fabbro*), and the life-long influence of Pound on Williams is too obvious for comment.⁴ Following Whitman, Pound carries metrical innovation to an extraordinary degree, and in roughly the same direction, getting the same results, despite the fact that Whitman worked by ear only, whereas Pound worked both with his ear and with a learned understanding of a great variety of meters outside the usual limits of English verse. For instance, in his essay on Arnaut Daniel:

> And in *Sols sui* and in other canzos the verse is syllabic, and made on the number of syllables, not by stresses, and the making by syllables cannot be understood by those of Petramala, who imagine the language they speak was that spoken by Adam, and that one system of metric was made in the world's beginning, and has since existed without change. And some think if the stress fall not on every second beat, or the third, that they must have right before Constantine. And the art of En Ar. Daniel is not literature but the art of fitting words well with music, well-nigh a lost art . . .

Although Pound occasionally permitted his protégés to practice in iambic pentameter, his standard advice was his early advice: "Let the candidate fill his mind with the finest cadences he can discover, preferably in a foreign language, so that the meaning of the words may be less likely to divert his attention from the movement" ("A Retrospect"). A good deal of the prosodic difficulty of the *Cantos* is doubtless caused by Pound's own habit of moving from one meter to another, and from meter to prose. But his verse is not lawless, as Pound insists to William Carlos Williams (letter of 21 October

⁴ Unfortunately, Eliot has spent a lot of time concealing his and Pound's indebtedness to Whitman. It is difficult to imagine historical or critical judgments more plainly wrong than Eliot's assertions that "Pound owes nothing to Whitman" and (in the wake of Arnold) that "Whitman was a great prose writer" (in his introduction to *Ezra Pound: Selected Poems*; other remarks of the same tenor, a decade earlier, in *Ezra Pound: His Metric and Poetry*).

1908): "Sometimes I use rules of Spanish, Anglo-Saxon and Greek metric that are not common in the English of Milton's or Miss Austen's day." Plus French, Latin, Italian, Provençal, and doubtless Chaldaic.

Despite the eclecticism of Pound's metric, his underlying theory of meter is pure American pragmatism. "*Rhythm.*—I believe in an 'absolute rhythm,' a rhythm, that is, in poetry which corresponds exactly to the emotion or shade of emotion to be expressed. A man's rhythm must be interpretative, it will be, therefore, in the end, his own, uncounterfeiting, uncounterfeitable" ("A Retrospect"). Given this premise, Pound quickly enough found himself at sword's point with the English tradition. In a 24 April 1916 letter to Iris Barry he wrote:

> Re metre: what they call "metre" in English means for the most part "jambic." They have heard of other metres and tried a few, but if the music of the words and the feel of the mood are to have any relation, one *must* write as one feels. It may be only an old hankering after quantitative verse that is at the bottom of it. All languages I think have shown a tendency to lengthen the foot in one way or another, as they develop.

And given this trend of argument, Pound had to end in an anti-English posture: "I *still* think the best *mechanism* for breaking up the stiffness and literary idiom *is* a different metre, the god damn iambic magnetizes certain verbal sequences" (letter of 13 August 1934). "Rhythm MUST have meaning," he had written Harriet Monroe in January 1915. "It can't be merely a careless dash off, with no grip and no real hold to the words and sense, a tumpty tum tumpty tum tum ta."

While it is obvious that neither Whitman nor Pound is undisciplined or formless, it is also obvious that both men represent in American poetry the furthest reach of metrical rebellion, nationalistically inspired and accurately aimed against the parent culture. As Pound says in canto 81: "To break the pentameter, that was the first heave." Doubtless he was thinking of Whitman, who is repeatedly named in canto 80, but in the lines immediately preceding he quotes a letter from one of the leaders of the American Revolution (John Adams) to another (Thomas Jefferson who, incidentally, wrote a conventional treatise on English prosody), and the subject of the correspondence is political tyranny. It is no accident that our two greatest poets place their prosodic radicalism, directed against the order and regularity of English verse, in the context of American political thought. In the 1855 preface to *Leaves of Grass*, which has much to say about "liberty," both literary and political, Whitman pointedly remarked: "The poetic quality is not marshalled in rhyme or uniformity." "Uniformity" can only mean the regular or syllable-stress metric of his English predecessors and American contemporaries. As his poems show, he totally rejected their assumptions and usages. Many years after the fact, holding court in Camden, Whitman delivered himself as follows (disciple Traubel reporting): "I said to W.: 'I'm getting more and more dubious about rhyme and all that.' W. said: 'I got wholly dubious about rhyme long ago: as to the 'all that,' I dismiss it without a peradventure.'"

But our sense of the vital relationship between Whitman and Pound, which is indispensable to an understanding of the theory and history of American poetry, need not rest solely upon these parallels between their intentions and practices, no matter how impressive they are. We now have external evidence, in a 1909 essay which came to light in recent years, that Pound's poetic career began with specific emulation of Whitman:

I honor him for he prophesied me while I can only recognize him as a forebear of whom I ought to be proud. . . . When I write of certain things I find myself using his rhythms. . . . Mentally I am a Walt Whitman who has learned to wear a collar and a dress shirt (although at times inimical to both). Personally I might be very glad to conceal my relationship to my spiritual father and brag about my more congenial ancestry—Dante, Shakespeare, Theocritus, Villon, but the descent is a bit difficult to establish. And, to be frank, Whitman is to my fatherland . . . what Dante is to Italy. . . . Like Dante he wrote in the "vulgar tongue," in a new metric. The first great man to write in the language of his people.[5]

What could be simpler or more conclusive? The line from Whitman to Pound is the radical tradition of American poetry; the connection between them is quite as firm and unassailable as the *traditio* from Chaucer to Spenser to Milton, which was also, among other things, a line of language and metric with a powerful native bias.

Yet neither Whitman nor Pound has succeeded in establishing a continuing general norm for American metric; rather, they indicate one of its possible limits. Moreover, the radical tradition seems to possess a sort of built-in dissatisfaction with its own achievements. It figures. As Pound very sensibly wrote about Whitman in a 13 October 1912 letter to Harriet Monroe: "The 'Yawp' is respected from Denmark to Bengal, but we can't stop with the 'Yawp.' We have no longer any excuse for not taking up the complete art." Or in "The Renaissance" (1914): "No American poetry is of any use for the palette. Whitman is the best of it, but he never pretended to have reached the goal. He knew himself, and proclaimed himself

[5] There are observations to the same general effect in *Patria Mia* (written before 1913), but the best statements are obviously these, from the 1909 essay, reprinted in Herbert Bergman, "Ezra Pound and Walt Whitman," *American Literature*, XXVII (1955), 56-61. The essay is much more conveniently found in *Whitman, A Collection of Critical Essays*, ed. Roy Harvey Pearce (Englewood Cliffs, N.J.: Prentice-Hall, 1962), pp. 8-10. Pound's later deprecations of Whitman notwithstanding, I fail to see him ever *as poet* recanting this youthful dedication to the Whitman tradition.

'a start in the right direction.' He never said, 'American poetry is to stay where I left it'; he said it was to go on from where he started it." With all of this Whitman would heartily agree.

To get a comparable fix on Pound it is necessary to introduce a subsequent poet in the radical tradition, and that poet can only be William Carlos Williams. Generally Williams admires Pound's poetic line, but sometimes a little edginess creeps into the praise: "So far I believe that Pound's line in his *Cantos*—there is something *like* what we shall achieve. Pound . . . has made a pre-composition for us. Something which when later (perhaps) packed and realized in living, breathing stuff will (in its changed form) be the thing" (letter to Kay Boyle, [1932]). And then we chance upon a passage like this in *Paterson*, obviously an interchange between Pound and Williams:

P. Your interest is in the bloody loam but what
   I'm after is the finished product.

I. Leadership passes into empire; empire begets insolence;
   insolence brings ruin.

Here in strong language is the perpetual problem of the American radical tradition: always it must be striving, contending, and its very victories are constantly threatened with disaster.

Williams, who was a Poe man, is even harder on Whitman, whom he might have been expected to admire with few reservations or none. "Whitman was a magnificent failure. He himself in his later stages showed all the terrifying defects of his own method. . . . The [poetic] line must, as a minimum, have a well-conceived form within which modification may exist" (letter to Kay Boyle, [1932]). "Whitman was never able fully to realize the significance of his structural innovations. . . . Selection, structural selection was lacking" ("Against the Weather," 1939). "Whitman to me was an instrument, one thing: he started us on the course of our researches

22

into the nature of the line by breaking finally with English prosody. After him there has been for us no line. There will be none until we invent it. . . . As I say, he has (for me) only one meaning and that virtually a negative one. He cleaned [cleared?] decks, did very little else" (12 April 1950 letter to Henry Wells). That is indeed a dismal view of Whitman, and a slightly irrational one, since as both Whitman and Williams knew, the only way to overthrow an unwanted authority is to write better than the authority. It isn't so much that Williams has it in for Whitman, I think—unless he's unconsciously angry at Whitman for failing to provide an American norm—as it is that he is suffering the endemic dilemma of the radical tradition in American poetry. Remove the hated enemy, regularity, and all you have left is freedom, i.e., your own ear facing chaos. " 'Free verse' since Whitman's time has led us astray. . . . Whitman was right in breaking our bounds but, having no valid restraints to hold him, went wild. He didn't know any better. . . . Whitman, great as he was in his instinctive drive, was also the cause of our going astray. I among the rest have much to answer for. No verse can be free, it must be governed by some measure, but not by the old measure. There Whitman was right but there, at the same time, his leadership failed him. The time was not ready for it" ("On Measure—Statement for Cid Corman," 1954). And so the battle rages. "I must make the new meter out of whole cloth," Williams wrote Robert Lowell on 11 March 1952. Or again from the "Statement for Cid Corman": "We have no measure by which to guide ourselves except a purely intuitive one which we feel but do not name."

The reason for all this difficulty is fairly clear: a radical tradition predicated on antagonism requires something to rebel *against*—a conservative tradition either foreign or introjected—but in either case productive of continuing discomfort. The norm of American metric cannot possibly be defined by the Whitman-Pound tradition alone, nor by what that tradition opposes, but only by the dialectic between them. (Such dialectic is perhaps best illustrated in the poetry of T. S. Eliot.) Fortunately for the continuing survival of our poetry, that dialectic can never be entirely resolved. The experimental American poet is wonderfully trapped between desire and necessity: the desire to be totally free of the English poetic tradition, and the necessity of maintaining at least an uneasy peace with his medium, the English language, which still, however Americanized, ineradicably embodies the English poetic tradition.

It is no mere happenstance, then, but the logic of history (which is sometimes surprisingly pure) that the two explosive eruptions of American poetry (1855 and 1912) should be followed by long periods of gradually increasing conservatism, during which a succession of poets (some great, some small) carried American metric back nearer the traditional norms of English verse. The history of American poetry is the history of recurrent explosions, metrically centered, caused by the frustration of the American poet, who is and is not an English poet, who has free verse but doesn't always want it, alternating with longer periods of conciliation and consolidation. Behind this historical oscillation lies a certain development, for after each explosion the American poet (Williams excepted) returns to relative regularity with a diminished sense of discomfort, a greater feeling of freedom and mastery, broader possibility, wider choice. What Bryant in 1876 implied had always been true was in fact at the very time he wrote in the process of becoming true, but in a very different sense from what he intended, and in ways of which he was totally ignorant. Sometime between Whitman and Pound, the English tradition became—insofar as we care to use it—ours.

The Age of Growing Discomfort
and Inadequate Remedy

Hiawatha! Hiawatha!
Sweet Trochaic milk and water!
Milk and water Mississippi
Flowing o'er a bed of sugar!—
Through three hundred Ticknor pages,
With a murmur and a ripple,
Flowing, flowing, ever flowing—
Damn the river!—damn the poet!

CAROLINE TICKNOR, *Hawthorne and his Publisher*

SOMEBODY sent Hawthorne this parody in 1856. "Ask the fact for the form," as Emerson sagely advised in "Poetry and Imagination," or, from the point of view of historical investigation, ask the form for the fact. The crucial period in the history of American poetry is between Bryant and Whitman, the Age of Growing Discomfort and Inadequate Remedy. Except for Lowell, who was notoriously too facile for his own good, the poets of this age are almost unbelievably inept in their metrics; and the more ambitious, the more inept (except for a brilliant hit like "The Raven"). Even Lowell, for all his over-facility in facile metrics (of which he was so vain), is frequently very uncertain in this respect, especially in *A Fable For Critics,* as Poe noted in his review of it, responding, conceivably, to Lowell's charge in that poem that Poe talked "like a book of iambs and pentameters,/ In a way to make people of common sense damn metres." It will be noticed, first, that Lowell's objection to Poe's always harping on metric is itself metrically inept (and not by design, either), and, second, that whenever a poet of this period desires to insult a peer he nearly always does so on the

25

score of metric. (In his *Fable*, Lowell also called Emerson's verse "not even prose.") All the evidence suggests that the metrical problem was insistently pressing and not in the way of solution.

Poe, for one, was always riding to a lather what he called his "favorite horse of versification," not only in his most considered definition of poetry as *"The Rhythmical Creation of Beauty,"*[6] but to more effect in his practical criticism, where his endless zeal for prosecuting metrical malefactors according to "the laws of verse, which are the incontrovertible laws of melody and harmony" (critique of Fitz-Greene Halleck, September 1843) sufficiently indicates his uneasiness. In the course of giving Bryant a thoroughgoing prosodic inspection (January 1837) he wrote: "Upon a rigid attention to minutiæ such as we have pointed out, any great degree of metrical success must altogether depend." His favorite words for lines he liked were "sweet" and "smooth"; for lines he didn't like, "rough" and "loose." His highest praise of another poet's versification was to call it "correct." Thus he moved readily from practice to principle: "In common with a very large majority of American, and, indeed, of European poets, Mrs. [Elizabeth Oakes] Smith seems to be totally unacquainted with the principles of versification —by which, of course, we mean its *rationale*. Of technical *rules* on the subject there are rather more than enough in our prosodies, and from these abundant rules are deduced the abundant blunders of our poets" (December 1845). Sadly, the indictment fits Poe him-

---

[6] Taken by itself, the phrase is uncomfortably ambiguous, for it might equally mean only "a beautiful creation which is rhythmical" or "beauty created by—instigated by, promoted by—rhythm." The following passage, from Poe's 1843 review of Griswold's *Poets and Poetry of America*, may perhaps help fix his probable meaning (or perhaps not): "POETRY, in its most confined sense, is *the result of versification*, but may be more properly defined as *the rhythmical personification of existing or real beauty*. One defines it as the 'rhythmical *creation* of beauty;' but though it certainly is a 'creation of beauty' in itself, it is more properly a personification, for the poet only personifies the image previously created by his mind."

self, both as prosodist and poet. No more than the other blunderers could he discriminate rule from rationale. However sensitive Poe may have been in other respects, in metric he appears to be quite confused by the desperation of his historical problem. Repeatedly he complained about all those iambic pentameters, but his usual answer to the problem was to complicate it with the introduction of meters even more artificial. As in his criticism he increasingly tried by the autocracy of pure reason to reduce traditional English metric to an exact science, the meters of his own poems became ever more *outré*. (See "The Rationale of Verse," a model of theoretical frustration, and such prosodic *tours de force* as "The Bells.") Poe had a good poetic instinct, and a good ear, but he was often metrically confused and distraught, responding to the American poetic situation with a kind of controlled hysteria which he alternatively sought to suppress by fiat or escape through "originality" (mechanical fussing with inessential details, alliteration, internal rhyme, refrains, trochaic jogs, anapestic romps). He was never to realize that only through a violent break with English tradition might he relieve his discomfort. This failure of perception is probably why his poetry so seldom fulfilled its promise—as Poe himself conceded, pleading lack of time.

> "Whose criticisms?" asked Emerson [of his young visitor from the West, William Dean Howells, who subsequently recorded the joke in his literary memoirs].
> "Poe's," I said again.
> "Oh," he cried out, after a moment, as if he had returned from a far search for my meaning, "*you mean the jingle-man!*"

The sage was obviously trying to dissociate himself from Poe, and to discredit the verses which Whitman would later call "melodious" and "morbid." (But that is not the extent of Whitman's response to Poe. See chapters two and three.) Typically, he insulted Poe's

27

metric. Yet Emerson was not so purely Poe's opposite number as he liked to think. Here is a poet of perhaps about equal talent who also finds it nearly impossible to write good poems, who must needs endlessly "experiment," who almost never experiments to any successful purpose, and whose most ambitious efforts regularly collapse on the rhythmical front. In a personal letter (17 October 1843) criticizing Emerson's "Ode to Beauty," Thoreau defines the trouble with his customary acuity and candor: "The tune is altogether unworthy of the thoughts. You slope too quickly to the rhyme, as if that trick had better be performed as soon as possible or as if you stood over the line with a hatchet. . . . It sounds like a parody." More generously, Theodore Parker mused in "The Writings of Ralph Waldo Emerson" (1850), "In Emerson's poetry there is often a ruggedness and want of finish which seems wilful in a man like him." Whether we go for candor or generosity makes no difference, the result is the same. Like the other American poets before Whitman, Emerson could be metrically conventional or he could dare to be (but with what trepidation) a little different. Either way—certain brilliant lines excepted—he ended by sounding like a travesty of his transatlantic betters, whether of the nineteenth or of the seventeenth century.

Nearly every ambitious American poem before 1855 reveals this same unease in relation to the traditional techniques, and especially the traditional metric, of English poetry. The awkwardness is not the deliberate and therefore successful awkwardness of "Philomela," nor the deliberate and therefore successful dissonance of *Paterson*. If the poems do not sound right, it is because the poets are trying to sound like English poets, and not getting away with it, or self-consciously trying to sound like American poets, without having any adequate idea, or auditory sense, what an American poet might sound like. For the most part, they do not sound like poets at all, as Emerson confessed, when he wrote in a personal letter of 1 February 1835: "My singing be sure is very 'husky,' &

is for the most part in prose. [Was he alluding to his essays or his poems?] Still am I a poet." Inversions are not poetry. Later, and even more pathetically, to Thomas Carlyle: ". . . not a poet but a lover of poetry, and poets, and merely serving as writer, &c. in this empty America, before the arrival of the poets."

Emerson and the Meter-Making Argument

It is dark here under ground, it is not evil or pain here,
it is blank here, for reasons.

WHITMAN, "The Sleepers"

EMERSON not only recognized Whitman the minute he arrived; by coming closer than any other writer to articulating the poetic problem for American culture, he more or less precipitated Whitman. In "The Poet," after complaining of those minor versifiers for whom "the argument is secondary, the finish of the verses is primary" (Poe?), he declared: "It is not metres, but a metre-making argument that makes a poem." At that moment American poetry cracked wide open. That Emerson was thinking of American poetry—and not of "romantic" or "modern" poetry, or poetry in general—is borne out by his subsequent elaboration in the same essay of that brilliant (if slightly ambiguous) phrase. "We have yet had no genius in America, with tyrannous eye, which knew the value of our incomparable materials [catalogue follows]. . . . Yet America is a poem in our eyes . . . and it will not wait long for metres. If I have not found that excellent combination of gifts in my countrymen which I seek, neither could I aid myself to fix the idea of the poet by reading now and then in Chalmers's collection of five centuries of English poets." Thus by 1844 at least one American poet was face to face with his poetic problem, clearly identified as both metrical and political. And neither his American colleagues nor his British predecessors were of the slightest use to him. The American poet had finally come to the end of his tether; plainly, that tether would have to be broken. Emerson defined the problem and sounded the call; Whitman broke the tether.

"Metre-making argument": the greatness of that phrase lies in the way it enables us to bring into single focus the metrical and cultural problems of American poetry, considered as a whole, by joining in exactly the right relationship American nationality (as in the prompting matter of American life, or even in the more broadly political intention to create a specifically American poetry) and an answering technique. America—by which we must understand the typical situation of the poet in this country—is the "argument" (the substance and the intention) which "makes" the meters appropriate to it. Subsequently, of course, as Emerson failed to add, probably because he took it for granted, the meters make the actual American poems which slowly begin to create that national sensibility and culture out of which further meters may arise, in order that poets may continue to sharpen and articulate and stabilize a developing sense of community. (Sometime listen to the progression of tones from "The Raven" to "Out of the Cradle Endlessly Rocking" to *The Waste Land* to *The Pisan Cantos* to *Paterson* and thence into our current Williams-inspired verse.) Because of the American Revolution, there is of course an obvious difference between English and American poetry, but it is probably sentimental to dwell overmuch on the natural and easy development of the English poetic tradition in comparison with the American poets' conspicuous discomfort and struggle and self-conscious intentions. We see these things clearly in our poetry because it is so recent, and because it is so much ourselves. Because the English tradition was initiated so long ago, we tend to overlook the likelihood that the creation by such poets as Chaucer and Spenser of the English heroic line (that great *bête noire* of the American songsters) was quite as difficult and self-conscious an affair as Whitman's liberation of American metric from foreign domination. The important difference is that the English poet, for all the difficulty of his technical problem, was at least in sensibility and culture one with a people

31

who were scarcely able to remember a time when they had not been a people (and even if they had been unable to remember, they could always make it up with King Arthur). The Americans had simultaneously to create their poetry and themselves. "Among a democratic people poetry will not be fed with legendary lays or the memorials of old traditions," Tocqueville predicted in the midst of the Age of Growing Discomfort and Inadequate Remedy. "All these resources fail him; but Man remains, and the poet needs no more" ("Of Some Sources of Poetry Among Democratic Nations"). As American poetry has subsequently and handsomely proved.

With Emerson's insight that verse techniques are for the most part the effects of poetic motives, and not, as Poe seems to have thought, their direct and mechanical causes, together with his understanding (if only tentative and partial) that the relation between meter and culture could not possibly be quite the same as in England, but must equally depend on a national literary situation, American poetry was in a position to make its first major breakthrough. And perhaps the most amazing thing about Emerson's insight is that more than a century later it remains as true as it ever was, if not truer. The longer American poetry goes on, the more complicated it gets, the more difficult it becomes for the historian to articulate a coherent theoretical understanding of it, the more obvious it seems that Emerson's way of defining the American problem in poetry is not merely the best, but the only way of defining it. Let me drive that point home in the fewest possible words by restating Emerson's fundamental proposition in terms of the Aristotelian theory of form, and from the vantage point of today. The *efficient cause* of "our poetry" is the whole group of American poets, radical and conservative, taken ensemble (the gangs of kosmos), or better, taken dialectically; the *material cause* is the dilemma of American poetry, caught between the desire for cultural freedom and equality and the necessities of language (including the

32

incorporation of poetic tradition); the *formal cause* is the total and exceedingly various response to this challenge actually made by the American poets; the *final cause* is the fact that an unmistakably American poetry now exists. Such an explanation, oriented toward the overriding question of metric (both poetically and nationalistically considered), seems to me to cover the ground, including, as it does, the poets, their problem, their poetic responses to it, and, finally, the entire field of American poetry, and to provide the best practical and realistic basis for a theory capable of eliciting an intelligible history of the art of poetry in this country.

Radical Explosions and Conservative Reassertions

The bird would cease and be as other birds
But that he knows in singing not to sing.
The question that he frames in all but words
Is what to make of a diminished thing.

ROBERT FROST, "The Oven Bird"

BY A KIND of historical logic, which would of course include the impact of Emerson's ideas on Whitman, the period of metrical discomfort was consummated by the first major explosion, or reflex,[7] of American poetry, *Leaves of Grass*. This explosion was in turn followed by a long period of conservative reassertion. In their metrics, Dickinson, Lanier, Moody, Robinson, even the much younger Frost more nearly resemble Bryant, Lowell, Poe, and Emerson than Whitman, but they no longer sound so awkward, so ill at ease in their meters, even when the meters are most in the English tradition. Emily Dickinson refurbished the old common measure so sensitively (and yet with a marvelous American harshness) as to earn for herself a place in several anthologies as the first modern American poet. Perhaps no other contemporary poet handles so wide a variety of traditional forms with such unobtrusive mastery as Frost, a feat all the more impressive in view of the fact that his theoretical understanding of the metrical problem shows little or no advance over Bryant. The poet, he says, "has been brought up by ear to choice of

---

[7] In *Patria Mia*, Pound calls Whitman a "reflex" and himself, by implication, another. "Whitman was not an artist, but a reflex, the first honest reflex, in an age of papier-mache letters. . . . [But] his 'followers' go no further than to copy the defects of his style. They take no count of the issue that an honest reflex of 1912 will result in something utterly different from the reflex of 1865."

34

two metres, strict iambic and loose iambic" ("The Constant Symbol"). The point is that Frost's poetry, however "regular," is also relaxed and rhythmically supple. It probably scans closer to Shakespeare than to Whitman, but it does not sound at all like the Bryant-machine cranking out second-hand Wordsworth; neither has it any of the uncomfortable, tormented awkwardness of Poe and Emerson. For instance, the opening lines of "After Apple-Picking":

> My long two-pointed ladder's sticking through a tree
> Toward heaven still,
> And there's a barrel that I didn't fill
> Beside it, and there may be two or three
> Apples I didn't pick upon some bough.
> But I am done with apple-picking now.

That is not the poetry of the American radical tradition, nor is it British poetry either. It is the representative mode of the American conservative line.

Predictably, there has been a psychological revolution between Bryant and Frost, and the difference is the existence of a Walt Whitman in the middle. Once the American poet knew freedom was available, and where to look for it, constraint was no longer constraining. The traditional meters were no longer exclusively English, the rhythms of our old home or our mortal enemy, nor absolutely inescapable either, though choice might still be affected by *Zeitgeist*. In 1892, Edwin Arlington Robinson, then a neophyte poet, wrote an elegy on Whitman, nostalgically, and perhaps too passively, contrasting the freedom and energy of the poetic situation then and now. Robinson's poem hauntingly suggests at least a half-hearted inclination to follow in the Whitman tradition, together with a mild sense of frustration that the times should prevent his doing so. Although his elegy was in blank verse, he singled out for praise Whitman's "piercing and eternal cadence." ("Too pure for us," he added.) That cadence was not to be "eternal" for him. In 1900, working on what he was always to consider his most experimental poem, *Captain Craig*, he was pleased to announce that it ended with a brass band and opened with a line that didn't scan. (It does, but just barely.) From that point on, his meters and his matter became less piercing. But at least he had a choice.

So the first period of conservative reassertion ran into the sand, as might have been predicted, to be followed, in the years around 1912, by a second major radical explosion. This time the force of the explosion was greater, because Pound had at his disposal not only his own power but Whitman's flowing through him; more efficiently directed toward a more stringently conceived poetic achievement, because Pound had learned much from Whitman's mistakes; more widespread, not only for these two reasons but because the poets affected by Pound were more disposed to be affected than Whitman's contemporaries had been. Pound's "heave" ("to break the pentameter") was not, after all, the first heave but the second. On the other hand, the Poundian revolution also met a powerful resistance, of a sort quite different from what prevented Whitman's example being followed in the mid-nineteenth century. As Bryant's attitudes indicate, Whitman was rejected mainly because he failed to conform to standards of metrical decorum assumed to be universally binding on all poets using the English language. By 1912, metrical regularity had been thoroughly introjected into American poetry and was therefore a viable alternative native tradition; embedded within the American sensibility, more or less purified of its noxious "English" implications, it proved a worthy opponent. Thus the succession of poets after Pound—Williams, Eliot, Crane, Ransom, Stevens, Roethke, Lowell—shows Pound's example first being imitated, then assimilated, then modified, then causing a considerable discomfort of its own. The poets began gradually to return to the time-honored norms of English metric, no longer buttressing themselves with "English" authority but taking heart from American examples. The early couplet poetry of Robert Lowell, for instance, seems to come mainly from the metrical usages of Robert Frost. So the process of Americanization goes on. "Mr. Lowell appears to be restrained by the lines; he appears to *want* to break them" (1951 review). Williams, who was not at that time of Mr. Lowell's party, could still read sensitively across the party barriers. On an even better occasion, he spoke of early Lowell: "His style should have been repugnant to me —but it wasn't. The American virus was in his veins. . . . His rhymed couplets, incongruous as they seemed, had a naive [native?] quality about them that attracted me. You couldn't call them or him English. . . . The line he uses is certainly not Pope" (*I Wanted to Write a Poem*, 1958).

This was the second, and much more powerful, conservative reassertion. In thirty years American poetry returned from Pound, whose Imagist manifesto demanded composition according to the musical phrase (and to hell with the metronome), to Wallace Stevens, with his "Virgilian cadences, up down,/ Up down," which sounds almost eighteenth century. As Stevens adds, not quite on our subject but nearly, "It is a war that never ends." It is the inevitable American civil war between meter like this (still quoting the conclusion of "Notes Toward a Supreme Fiction"):

> Soldier, there is a war between the mind
> And sky, between thought and day and night. It is
> For that the poet is always in the sun

and meter like this (from another war poem, *The Pisan Cantos*):

> Whitman liked oysters
> at least I think it was oysters
>   and the clouds have made a pseudo-Vesuvius
>   this side of Taishan
> Nenni, Nenni, who will have the succession?

37

Dateline 1973: it looks as if Williams has the succession. But not forever. Bearing in mind the historical dialectic of American poetry, it would be sheer idiocy either to undervalue the continuing power of the conservative tradition, or to be caught sleeping at our posts when the next great radical bomb goes off.

The United States as a Poem

> But, creature of the weather, I
> don't want to go any faster than
> I have to go to win.
>
> Music it for yourself.
>
> WILLIAMS, *Paterson*

LIKE all his countrymen provincially cut off from the centers of the older and parent civilizations, the American poet is periodically compelled to assume the defiant stance, to ward off too much—too much of the wrong kind of—influence. This is obvious in the poems and prefaces of Whitman and in most American poems and prefaces down to Williams and beyond. Yet Whitman's poems and prefaces also insistently proclaim the American poet's need to involve himself with Europe and the rest of the world. Few poets have regarded their forerunners, especially the greatest ones— all of them European—whom we might have expected him to fear, with more generosity or with a more fraternal affection. Pound's devoted search for models through all cultures in all ages shows the same generosity, but also, when you think about it, the same animus as Whitman's smashing of English metric. A plethora of models (few of them English) is an excellent way of fending off the tradition whose closeness makes it dangerous. But the generosity of Whitman and Pound stems primarily from their greatness, which is their radicalism, the greatness that belongs only to those with sufficient daring (and ability) to be wholly themselves. Poe, who was torn by convention, despised the best poets of the past. Poor Emerson found them short of his "ideal." "Milton is too literary, and Homer too literal and historical" ("The Poet").

But Whitman, Pound, and, *a fortiori*, the more conservative poets are still more deeply implicated in European—specifically English

—tradition than these merely cultural or emulative considerations imply. As usual in the arts, this more practical and realistic involvement arises from the medium, and is thus, once again, most readily seen in metric. The American poet may mutter to himself, "and as for those who deform thought with iambics," as Pound does in canto 98 (the ghost of Whitman cheering him on), yet Pound no less than Whitman is frequently caught deforming thought with what sound suspiciously like iambics: in the *Cantos*, for example, "To have gathered from the air a live tradition/ or from a fine old eye the unconquered flame"; in *Leaves of Grass*, for example, "As fill'd with friendship, love complete, the Elder Brother found,/ The Younger melts in fondness in his arms." It appears that even those who campaign most actively against iambics find it desirable to return to them from time to time, quite often because of a temporarily conciliatory mood toward the traditions they customarily oppose (as suggested by these quotations), but nearly always, ironically, for their most splendid effects, high emotion or the climax of an argument. In "Song of the Exposition," a poem beautifully blending Whitman's aspirations for an American poetry with his passionate adoration of the European past ("Not to repel or destroy so much as accept, fuse, rehabilitate"), a long passage of loose and falling rhythm, which is not only markedly (and I think deliberately) anti-English in technique, but also includes the flat statement that "the stately rhythmus of Una and Oriana" is "ended," surprisingly concludes with a sudden reversion to English regularity (iambic tetrameter): "Blazon'd with Shakspere's purple page,/ And dirged by Tennyson's sweet sad rhyme."

Yet, and therefore, even the radical poet is lured back time and again toward the metrical usages he professes to despise (because he fears them) by his ingrained respect for the English tradition. The poems of Chaucer, Sidney, Spenser, Shakespeare, Donne, Milton, Dryden, Pope, Wordsworth, Tennyson, Browning, Hopkins, Yeats, to name only a few, quite apart from their more obvious use as "cultural heritage," press upon the American poet realistically, as measures, forms, and words. Despite his Revolutionary antagonism, poems sound that way; or, more accurately, since we increasingly possess poems of our own that do not sound quite that way, that is what poems may sound like, or have sounded like. They will never sound that way again, and yet, on the other hand, the sound will never die out as long as the printing presses continue to operate. Literally hundreds of these poems are too good to be ignored or rejected. Among the answers to the question, "What do you hear Walt Whitman?" (in "Salut au Monde!"), we find the telltale evidence, and indeed the entire theory of American poetry: "I hear continual echoes from the Thames." Perhaps that is one reason why Eliot in *The Waste Land* admonishes that "sweet" river to "run softly" till he ends his song. "Until I end my song," Pound chimes in (canto 74).

It goes without saying that the American poet can never abandon the English language either, nor radically modify it, except as the speech of his own people may in the course of centuries modify it. He can listen to the changes, and ring them, but he cannot cause them: medium is dependent on culture, and the world-shaking poet is dependent on both. The major poet is perforce a modest chap. But a great variety of American poets are always trying to outrun natural development. I have already alluded to the fact that Whitman's fondness for falling rhythm is an obviously anti-English gesture. "Out of the cradle endlessly rocking,/ Out of the mockingbird's throat, the musical shuttle." Out of that musical shuttle, and often with a little mockery, or self-mockery, American poetry has recurrently tried to rock. Even Longfellow had given us, eight years before *Leaves of Grass*, such an imperishable public-school line as "This is the forest primeval. The murmuring pines and the hemlocks" (for which intransigence trochee-loving Poe promptly rapped his knuckles in the revised version of "The Rationale of Verse"). Significantly, we hear of Longfellow temporarily putting aside falling rhythm in the thick of composition, to try how *Evangeline* might sound in iambic pentameter couplets, but quickly returning to his dactyls. Neither Whitman, Pound, nor Eliot, of course, would ever commit the error of writing an entire poem in a meter so awkward and unnatural. But used sparingly, flexibly, and with genuine delicacy, as Whitman so often uses it, falling rhythm is undeniably one of the most rewarding metrical maneuvers for the American poet. Simply because it strikes the ear—even the American ear—as unusual, it immediately frees him from his nervous apprehension of being overwhelmed by English lilt, and leads to his dearly beloved dissonance and looseness. Perhaps American metric is never so enticing as when a basically rising rhythm is overlaid with heavily falling cadences and loaded with trochaic and dactylic words. All considerations of "rising" and "falling" fade from the mind as the ear responds to a rhythm absolutely *sui generis*; for example, in the opening lines of the *Cantos:*

> And then went down to the ship,
> Set keel to breakers, forth on the godly sea, and
> We set up mast and sail on that swart ship,
> Bore sheep aboard her, and our bodies also
> Heavy with weeping, and winds from sternward
> Bore us out onward with bellying canvas,
> Circe's this craft, the trim-coifed goddess.

Indeed the craft is Circean, for the passage begins regularly enough and only gradually transforms itself into another movement. The same American music is everywhere in Eliot:

> Where is there an end of it, the soundless wailing,
> The silent withering of autumn flowers
> Dropping their petals and remaining motionless;

42

Where is there an end to the drifting wreckage,
The prayer of the bone on the beach, the unprayable
Prayer at the calamitous annunciation?

(Paradoxically, this passage from "The Dry Salvages" also loosely imitates the age-old sestina.)

"'My bikini is worth yr/ raft'" (Leucothoe, as quoted by Pound). The greatest metrical moments of American poetry customarily arise from this tension between the American poet's desire respectfully to wrench the English tradition out of its course and the disinclination of the English tradition, or the English language, to be too rudely forc'd. Except on rare occasions, iambic pentameter does not work very well in this country. Yet falling rhythm equally fails except as offset or overlay of a generally rising rhythm. Introduction of too many unstressed syllables in rising rhythm does not really eliminate iambic meter but conducts to plain prose. So, beyond a certain point, does too reckless a mixture of rising and falling feet. Nor can the American poet write entirely in spondees, though sometimes it sounds as if he were trying to. A similar tension manifests itself in line length. The standard line length for serious poetry in English is five feet, as any anthology quickly confirms. But taken as a whole, American poets give a queer impression of being exceedingly anxious to run to either extreme in order to avoid what obviously seems to them an oppressive, or prescriptive, norm. The unduly short line is a common American phenomenon as early as Emerson and Thoreau; it recurs in Dickinson and in Imagism. Conversely, the inordinately long line is a common American phenomenon as early as Bryant and Poe and Longfellow, and is, of course, the hallmark of most of Whitman and Pound, and much of Eliot. Yet a surprising number of fine American poems are five-stress, and in times of conservative reassertion, pentameter easily and naturally establishes itself as the accepted length (Robinson, Stevens). Tetrameter and hexameter lines tend to break in the middle. Trimeters are too gnomic, fourteeners too walloping, for most poetic purposes.

Obviously there are a great number of other prosodic factors at work, constraining and annoying and stimulating the American poet, but even these brief remarks may suggest in what practical sense we are entitled to say that the American poet may never entirely escape his metrical past, nor ever rest entirely easy in it, though he tends to rest easier as he gradually assimilates it to his own needs and purposes. The American poet has not been able to resolve his dilemma, and our frequent wish that he might—that he once and for all achieve a purely "American" solution of poetic problems—is a foolish chauvinistic wish. If it is impossible for our poets to innovate as freely as some of them would like, it is equally impossible for them to continue humming the same old monotone, as too many modern British poets do. If it is a meter-making argument we want—that is, a literary situation incessantly pressing toward the improbable resolutions of rhythm and harmony and form, out of the most intractable materials—then we are lucky enough. A meter-making argument is exactly what the American poet has as his birthright, because that is what America, poetically speaking, is. Possibly that is what Whitman meant when, following Emerson, he referred to the United States as essentially the greatest poem. At the end of his career, in "A Backward Glance O'er Travel'd Roads," he said it more plainly: "I consider 'Leaves of Grass' and its theory experimental—as, in the deepest sense, I consider our American republic itself to be, with its theory." But experiment, in poetry as in politics, is valuable only insofar as it leads to practicable and pluralistic actualities—not *modus* but *modi vivendi*—and under the constant pressure of change. This is the real achievement of American poetry: that the desperate experiments of our poets, tormented by a deep-seated conflict between loyalty to culture and to medium, have in the course of time eventuated in a specifically American tradition, a spectrum of possibility that is neither the English way nor its opposite, but both, in provocative antithesis and alternation, and occasionally, on halcyon days, in strange and delightful harmony. And yet a harmony continuously on the verge of dissolution and re-articulation, so that even as we try to fix its essence in a dialectic formula, American poetry is almost certainly undergoing a further metamorphosis.

Chapter Two

THE CONSTITUTING METAPHOR

Whitman and Metaphorical Form

One simple trail of idea, epical, makes the poem.

WHITMAN, "Preparatory Reading and Thought"

HOWEVER complex and subtle they are in reality—for no two lines of verse ever have exactly the same rhythm, even when they have precisely the same words; how could they, when they occur at different times in the poem?—at least in general outline the problems of American meter are relatively simple. In comparison, the problem of American metaphor is what any good American poet would call a fair bitch. (And poetic diction is worse.) We can, if we must, start a bit back, with an obvious concessive point: American metaphors, like American meters, are sometimes just like anybody else's. When even Whitman—great unapproachable guru—in "Out of the Cradle Endlessly Rocking" speaks of "white arms out in the breakers tirelessly tossing," we have (at least we think we have) the kind of metaphor with which we are familiar in dozens of other poets, mainly British. Whitman's major metaphors are not local metaphors like that, but overall, generative metaphors that constitute whole poems or poetries. Inevitably so: you can't write poems in a poetry that hasn't yet been invented; you have to make up its forms as you go along. The American model for metaphor had to be grandiose in scope, and for the Romantic Americans there was an obvious lead. Of the *Inferno*, Whitman remarked in *Notes and Fragments*, encapsulating the whole theory of American metaphor: "It is a short poem. . . . Mark the simplicity of Dante, like the Bible's—different from the tangled and florid Shakespeare. Some of his idioms must, in Italian, cut like a knife. He narrates like some short-worded, superb, illiterat— an old farmer or some New England blue-light minister. . . . Mark,

49

I say, his economy of words—perhaps no other writer ever equal to him. One simple trail of idea, epical, makes the poem—all else resolutely ignored. This alone shows the master. In this respect [Dante] is the most perfect in all literature. A great study for diffuse moderns." (Those remarks are also a great study of how difficult it is to separate metaphor from diction in the theory of American poetry.) In the twentieth century, in *The Spirit of Romance*, Pound echoes Whitman: "The *Divina Commedia* is a single elaborated metaphor." Despite the many difficulties with the unity of his own long poem, this is standard doctrine in Pound. As he writes in *Guide to Kulchur*: "the aim of technique is that it establish the totality of the whole. The total significance of the whole"; "the *forma*, the immortal *concetto*, the concept, the dynamic form which is like the rose pattern driven into the dead iron-filings by the magnet."

It is this simple trail of idea about one simple trail of idea that furnishes the key to Whitman's constituting metaphors, though in retrospect it seems odd that we have been unable to open them equally with Whitman's titles.[1] "It is a profound, vexatious, never-explicable matter," he wrote in *Specimen Days* ("Cedar-Plums Like—Names"), "this of names," meaning titles. "I have been exercised deeply about it my whole life." That is not strictly true, but it leads to the truth. The truth is that we have not yet given enough

---

[1] His earlier readers seem to have been more aware of Whitman's typical metaphorical forms than we are. See, e.g., Oscar Triggs, in "The Growth of 'Leaves of Grass'" (1902), after quoting Whitman's preparatory notes for "Song of the Broad-Axe": "Here it is evident, as Dr. Bucke has pointed out, the idea of the poem came to him as a whole and instantaneously. He took the piece of paper and jotted down an outline which would serve to call up the image again to his mind. By the aid of the memorandum of the initial inspiration he wrote later the poem as he first conceived it. Words and phrases, the names of things and processes, had to be thought out and hunted up. In the outline he indicates also certain matters that he must investigate. His papers show that this was his usual method of composition."

attention to the collocation of such curious facts as the complete absence of titles in the edition of 1855—more literally, most of the poems are called "Leaves of Grass," until near the end, as if Whitman had run out of type, when they are simply headed by a double space bar—and the nearly parallel titling of 1856, together with the later fussing over titles ("Song of Myself" and "Out of the Cradle Endlessly Rocking" are the most notorious examples). In 1855, everything or nothing. By 1856, something like this (I quote half the titles of the Table of Contents; the other half is virtually the same):

> Poem of Walt Whitman, an American
> Poem of Women
> Poem of Salutation
> Broad-Axe Poem
> Poem of a Few Greatnesses
> Poem of the Body
> Poem of Many in One
> Poem of You, Whoever You Are
> Poem of the Road
> Poem of Procreation
> Poem of the Poet
> Clef Poem
> Poem of The Singers, and of The Words of Poems
> Poem of Perfect Miracles
> Poem of the Propositions of Nakedness
> Poem of The Sayers of The Words of The Earth

The titles are like so many grammatical equations in which the substantive is steady and only the attribute varies. Whitman was fumbling out a theory of the constituting metaphor: the attribute, the simple trail of idea, would be not only the individual poem

51

itself, but as in Dante the *concetto*, the simple trail of idea that would form, ordain, and establish the poem.[2]

The greatest Whitman poems are unified by a single overriding metaphor, often dialectic, stated or implied by the title or by the poem as a whole, or by both, to which the particular, localized elements of the poem ideally conform. Thus we may explain in simplest terms how apparently prose statements, too often taken as such, are rather the fragmented, faceted aspects of the constituting metaphor. It is well worth recalling, as Whitman so often did, how Whitman's United States, one and many, singular and plural, were mysteriously constituted into "the Union" by a written document that in a dark hour proved as tenuous as his own. "Finally, as I have lived in fresh lands," Whitman wrote in the 1876 Centennial preface, "inchoate, and in a revolutionary age, future-founding, I have felt to identify the points of that age, these lands, in my recitatives, altogether in my own way. Thus my form has strictly grown from my purports and facts, and is the analogy of them. Within my time the United States have emerg'd from nebulous vagueness and suspense, to full orbic, (though varied,) decision." The analogy between the Constitution and a Whitman poem is even more ob-

---

[2] There is a good deal of overlap between Whitman's formal conception of a poem and his formal conception of a lecture. Here are some notes to himself on the latter topic:

Style
A main requirement of any Lecture
Does it embody, and express (one leading and simple idea) fitted to popular apprehension without too much complication—and the accessories (and other ideas, in themselves, equally great, but, for the present purposes, not brought too forward) all carefully kept down so that the *strong colors, lights and lines of the Lecture* mark that *one simple leading idea or theory.*

Clifton J. Furness, *Walt Whitman's Workshop* (Cambridge, Mass., 1928), p. 36.

vious in an astonishing letter Whitman wrote *Harper's* magazine on 7 January 1860 about a poem he finally titled "Our Old Feuillage":

> The theory of *"A Chant of National Feuillage"* is to bring in, (devoting a line, or two or three lines, to each,) a comprehensive collection of touches, localés, incidents, idiomatic scenes, from every section, South, West, North, East, Kanada, Texas, Maine, Virginia, the Mississippi Valley, &c. &c. &c.—all intensely fused to the urgency of compact America, "America always"—all in a vein of graphic, short, clear, hasting along—as having a huge bouquet to collect, and quickly taking and binding in every characteristic subject that offers itself—making a compact, the-whole-surrounding, *National Poem*, after its sort, after my own style.
>
> Is there any other poem of the sort extant—or indeed hitherto attempted?[3]
>
> You may start at the style. Yes, it is a new style, of course, but that is necessitated by new theories, new themes—or say the new treatment of themes, forced upon us for American purposes. Every really new person, (poet or other,) *makes* his style—sometimes a little way removed from the previous models—sometimes very far removed.

Making a compact, the-whole-surrounding, *National Poem*. There is the single poem of constituting metaphor. But the same critical principle applies also to *Leaves of Grass* as a whole, which went through many editions over a period of many years, yet always retained its original title, which is the constituting metaphor (leaf of grass, leaf of a book) of the volume. ("Feuillage.") That Whit-

---

[3] Yes. In the same passage about Dante with which this chapter opens, Whitman, listing the main "points" of the *Inferno*, mentions first *"hasting on."* It seems quite evident that "hasting on" (or "hasting along") and "one simple trail of idea" were closely associated in Whitman's mind.

man's life-long title was itself a perpetually-expanding constituting metaphor for the various poems taken ensemble (during the same period the States were also expanding) is corroborated by two late remarks: "I have probably had an advantage in constructing from a central and unitary principle since the first" ("An Old Man's Rejoinder"); and again: "This ensemble idea haunts me till I get it realized in an identity volume" (letter of 13 October 1888).

The constituting metaphor constitutes the poem by constituting its being, its situation or context, its limits and grounds in reality. And it is precisely at this point that we need to exercise all our poetic delicacy of intuition, lest we interpret the subordinate details literally. Perhaps it falls out so in "Song of Myself," where all the subsidiary propositions are surely to be taken as localized metaphors of "selfhood" in general, and where Whitman's one error may have been in electing a metaphor too ambiguous, too diversely inclusive, to establish a firm order commanding the details. At least this much is obvious: The more representative Whitman poem eschews or minimizes the kind of localized metaphor like "white arms out in the breakers tirelessly tossing," which rather suggests the kind of metaphorical situation found in most British poems, namely a mixed series of plain statements and illustrative, extending, incarnating metaphors (frequently similes), or, alternatively, a mixed series of pure metaphors, which in the old critical parlance add up to more than the sum of their parts. Whitman preferred the single metaphor, one major metaphor to the poem, the poem conceived as the single metaphor articulated, the huge bouquet collected and tied, the simple trail of idea, the hasting on. Whitman's poems are analytic, while the usual English poem is markedly synthetic: "chasing one aborted conceit after another," Whitman scoffed in *Democratic Vistas* at the usual British-imitating nineteenth-century American poem.

Whitman was freer. So long as he remained responsible for the metaphorical implications of statement and image within the limits of the constituting situation, Whitman was able to say what he would, and as prosaically or imagistically as he liked. Conversely his statements and images almost automatically take from the constituting metaphor an unobtrusively figurative flavor, where the metaphorical value of each separate item need be no further asserted by the poem, however often it may need be asserted by the critic. Like Dante's Ulysses, Wallace Stevens sailed close, but failed the weather mark, when he wrote in "Three Academic Pieces": "In both prose and poetry, images come willingly but, usually, although there is a relation between the subject of the images there is no relation between the images themselves. A group of images in harmony with each other would constitute a poem within, or above, a poem." In Plato-land they might. In this country they constitute a poem, and neither within nor above.

Poe and the Analogue of the Short Story

It is the curse of a certain order of mind, that it can never rest satisfied with the consciousness of its ability to do a thing. Still less is it content with doing it. It must both know and show how it was done.

POE, "Marginalia"

WHITMAN'S closest predecessor in the constituting metaphor is, as we might expect, Poe. (It is just as surely not Emerson, who in respect to metaphor doggedly clings to the traditional British ways, despite his assertion in "The Poet" that "in the order of genesis the thought is prior to the form." See, for example, "Brahma," which has nearly as many metaphors as lines.) Constituting metaphors can of course be found here and there throughout the world's literature, and not only in Dante; but they can be found most easily, and nearest home, in the poems of Poe. "The Raven" (1845) and "Ulalume" (1847) are conspicuously the great American poems of Whitman's impressionable youth, and they are both conspicuously poems of constituting metaphor. Both are poems of pure situation, which is why Poe, in "The Philosophy of Composition," using a different and (to us) confusing terminology, could say that "the first metaphorical expression" of "The Raven" comes near the end; but he also said that the whole poem was a single "under-current, however indefinite, of meaning," to which the localized metaphor might serve as a kind of key.

In general, Poe's criticism shows a marked distaste for the British way of metaphor. Of Bulwer's *Night and Morning*, he wrote with asperity: he has "an absolute mania of metaphor—metaphor always running into allegory. Pure allegory is at all times an abomination. . . . Metaphor, its softened image, has indisputable force when sparingly and skilfully employed. Vigorous writers [like Poe in "The Raven"] use it rarely indeed" (April 1841). Granted, it is often exceedingly difficult to discover what Poe is driving at, but it seems sufficiently clear from these quotations that in his critical thought allegory (bad) and under-current (good) normally stand in some kind of opposition, and that metaphor is an ambivalent idea, bad when it leads to allegory or is simply stuck on as local decoration, good when it is subservient to, or even revelatory of, the under-current. It takes very little brainwork to translate the terms into Whitman's, thereby finding in Poe a close approximation to Whitman's sense of the constituting metaphor.

Both poets share a driving passion for unity of poetic ideas or forms. Here is Poe, in an adverse mood, chiding Longfellow: "He has no combining or binding force. He has absolutely nothing of unity. His brief pieces (to whose brevity he has been led by an instinct of the deficiencies we now note) abound in high thoughts, either positively insulated or showing these same deficiencies by the *recherché* spirit of their connection" (review of *Voices of the Night*, February 1840). Two years later, in a sweeter mood, here is Poe praising Longfellow on precisely the same ground where he had previously cut him down (Poe's inconsistency about Longfellow's poems is not at issue; possibly Longfellow had improved; the point is the absolute identity of aesthetic principle in two reviews that come to opposite conclusions): "Mr. Longfellow, very properly, has but one *leading* idea which forms the basis of his poem; but to the aid and development of this one there are innumerable others, of which the rare excellence is, that all are in keeping, that none could be well omitted, that each tends to the one general effect. It is unnecessary to say another word upon this topic" (review of *Ballads and Other Poems*, April 1842).

Despite many obvious differences between Poe's and Whitman's poems, their shared passion for unity sometimes works itself out in curiously parallel ways. As Whitman's remarks about Dante suggest, a constituting metaphor is rather more like a plot than an illustration, and indeed in "The Philosophy of Composition" Poe introduces his analysis of the under-current poem, "The Raven," with a general discussion of plot and unity of effect in the novel and the short story. Poe's insistence on unity of effect in fiction, as in poetry, and everything else, including the universe, and the way he drifted, or the market impelled him, from poetry to fiction to poetry again, almost certainly influenced his feeling for the constituting metaphor. (Whitman also did apprentice work in the short story before turning to serious poetry.) In "The Philosophy of Composition" the theory is drawn from fiction, but the specimen under examination is a poem, and there is neither any recognition of anomaly nor any critical transition from the one genre to the other:

> Nothing is more clear than that every plot, worth the name, must be elaborated to its *dénouement* before anything be attempted with the pen. [Huck Finn Whitman took no stock in this part of the injunction.] It is only with the *dénouement* constantly in view that we can give a plot its indispensable air of consequence, or causation, by making the incidents, and especially the tone at all points, tend to the development of the intention.
>
> There is a radical error, I think, in the usual mode of constructing a story. Either history affords a thesis—or one is suggested by an incident of the day—or, at best, the author sets himself to work in the combination of striking events to form merely the basis of his narrative—designing, generally, to fill in with description, dialogue, or autorial comment, whatever crevices of fact, or action, may, from page to page, render themselves apparent.
>
> I prefer commencing with the consideration of an *effect*.

So do the delegates to constitutional conventions, whereas Poe's account of "the usual mode of constructing a story" may to the irreverent sound like the typical muddle-through procedures of the usual nineteenth-century British poem. The key word is "intention," since it is intention that enables us to modulate from fictive effect to poetic form, as from poetry to politics.

It goes without saying that all successful works of art are unified; and also that there is no single nor simple way of unification. Poems may be unified in a variety of ways. Roughly speaking—very roughly speaking, for of course exceptions will be found—the unity of the nineteenth-century British poem comes from the tone, or, in other words, from poetic diction. But the American poets have no unified poetic diction to speak of—indeed, many a recent poet such as William Carlos Williams recoils in horror from the very idea—and are thereby obliged to find their unity elsewhere. Roughly speaking, they find it, when they find it at all, in the constituting metaphor that is the poetical complement of the fictional intention. In "The Philosophy of Composition," Poe first calls "The Raven" a "simple narrative." But then we come to a revelatory, localized metaphor, a facet or sign of the under-current, and the plot demonstrably thickens. "It will be observed that the words, 'from out my heart,' involve the first metaphorical expression in the poem." Metaphorical, of course, in Poe's special sense of the term. And then he gives us the whole secret of the poem: "They [these words], with the answer, 'Nevermore,' dispose the mind to seek a moral in all that has been previously narrated. The reader begins now to regard the Raven as emblematical—but it is not until the very last line of the very last stanza, that the intention of making him emblematical of *Mournful and Never-ending Remembrance* is permitted distinctly to be seen." There is the constituting metaphor of "The Raven" blazoned as plain as a billboard. (Yet it is also highly significant that the words "Mournful and Never-ending Remembrance" do not appear in the poem. Had Poe not told us, we would have to deduce his constituting metaphor by sheer poetic intuition.) The Raven as emblematical *is* the *dénouement* of the poem, and it is also the single metaphor

59

that constitutes the poem. "From out my heart" is the localized, faceted clue to the under-current or constituting metaphor. Poe's constituting metaphors are perhaps even more cunningly hidden than Whitman's (and just as seldom honored in Poe criticism), perhaps because they are so forthrightly flaunted by the situations, very much as in the placement of the purloined letter. (As Poe was fond of saying, the most profound truths usually lie open and on the surface, which is why nobody ever sees them.) We have been duped by the situations and missed the metaphors, and read the poems as claptrap. Claptrap is our national evasion of Poe as prose is our national evasion of Whitman.

In Which Power Transacts Itself

I read you all day
in white light changing.

Your voice cuts through
my worn-out ribbon.

The horizon sharpens.

EDWIN FUSSELL, "Looking Out"

"CROSSING BROOKLYN FERRY" is an excellent instance of Whitman's metaphorical forms. (In 1856 it was titled "Sun-Down Poem," which suggests that Whitman was not yet entirely clear in his mind what the poem was about. Naturally I am quoting the final version.) As usual, there are two ways to read it, the ordinary, pedantic way, in which everything is taken at face value, and the other, Dantean, poetic way, as a simple trail of idea. Read the first way, the poem comes out as a conglomeration of prosaic statements ("It avails not, time nor place—distance avails not"), which would then seem to require philosophical or biographical interpretation (exit poem), together with nonfigurative images ("sea-gulls . . . high in the air floating with motionless wings, oscillating their bodies"; a few lines later, "ships at anchor . . . the swinging motion of the hulls"), which would seem to resist interpretation entirely (exit reader). We are lost in the *selva oscura* and only Dante (Whitman's Dante) can lead us to the *diritta via*.

One simple trail of idea (which does not exclude dialectic), the single subsumed metaphor, yet not unduly arcane; most of the poem is implicit in its final title and in the opening line: "Flood-tide below me! I see you face to face!" Whitman's formal genius resides in the fact that once he achieves his constituting metaphor, then all

61

its amplifying, corroborative, qualifying facets automatically become submetaphorical variants and need not be further specified. Whitman, of course, could not have foreseen that he would later be read by Wallace Stevens, who wrote, apparently without a trace of self-doubt: "Whitman is disintegrating as the world, of which he made himself a part, disintegrates. 'Crossing Brooklyn Ferry' exhibits this disintegration" (letter of 8 February 1955).[4] This is literally reverse English. Stevens fails to sense that Whitman has reversed the standard meaning of the word "disintegrate"; as a result, Stevens inevitably reverses the meaning of the poem. A better reader (preferably not a poet or scholar—poets are too hung up on their own mannerisms to hear Whitman's and scholars are too obsessed with the search for absolute truth to hear anything) would have recognized that "disintegrate" is somehow part and parcel of the customary Whitman paradox of "simple separate person" and "En-Masse." But to stop there is to fall short of the ultimate poem. The customary-paradox reading simply cannot come to terms with lines like these:

> I too had been struck from the float forever held in solution,
> I too had receiv'd identity by my body.

Obviously there is much ebb and flow in the poem (another submetaphor of the oscillating motion through which the poem moves toward final creation), but ebb and flow are not exactly the same

[4] The probable cause of the misreading is that Stevens is himself a disintegrative poet. See his remarks about the lack of relation among images in a poem, quoted at the end of the first section of this chapter. In a letter of 13 July 1949 Stevens wrote: "I became interested in doing a poem, which, like most long poems, is merely a collection of short ones." It would appear that Stevens was unduly impressed by Poe's arguments against the long poem and unduly inattentive to Poe's equal (and somewhat contradictory) arguments for unity. In any case, it is obvious that Stevens does not compose within the tradition of the constituting metaphor.

thing as float, and float is not a possible metaphor for democratic society, and "struck" is also obscure.

Whitman reverses the meanings of words. He admits it in this very poem: "I too knitted the old knot of contrariety." He also changes the meanings of ordinary words. (Both of these word games are integral to the American vernacular, especially in slang. The relaxed common reader talks this way most of the time, which may explain why he can so frequently get at Whitman when the poet and scholar can't.) "Float" is one of Whitman's favorite changed words. It is his special metaphor for the undifferentiated future. It is the *future*, not the present (much less the past, which is fixed), which is "forever held in solution." When Whitman (Walter or Walt) was born, he was "struck" from the float, he received identity by his body (how else?), once and for all (Whitman was a devout believer in personal immortality, not so simple-minded an idea as many people like to suppose), and he was henceforth a person. Whitman is not disintegrating. He is *disintegrated*. So are all the other people in the poem:

> The simple, compact, well-join'd scheme, myself disintegrated,
>   every one disintegrated yet part of the scheme . . .

The progress of the poem is to move forward, past individuation, though retaining it, into a further aesthetic unity and communion. Past, present, and future whirl like a mobile in a high wind as Whitman himself probes into the float, projecting this poem toward readers who are still in the float ("I consider'd long and seriously of you before you were born"), meanwhile projecting himself past death into personal immortality:

> Who knows but I am enjoying this?
> Who knows, for all the distance, but I am as good as looking at
>   you now, for all you cannot see me?

63

And goes on talking. It is impossible to shut Whitman up. He has rearranged the universe to suit his own formal conveniences.

Ultimately the poem affirms that the poetical action of crossing Brooklyn Ferry is metaphorical for—and also, but not only, the real-life action of—certain analogous actions of human experience ("Others will enter the gates of the ferry and cross from shore to shore"), such as floats, rhythms, and passages. The poem is full of them. Now understanding a little about the float, we may begin to sense the metaphorical point of the gulls oscillating their bodies and the ships rolling their hulls. Rhythms? Most obviously between good and evil as in the sixth section (not to mention the oscillating form of the poem and Whitman's metric audacities). Passages? Mainly the ferry between present writer and future reader and im- mortal writer, etc., ad infinitum. "The white wake left by the pas- sage." Why so apparently inept an image in a poem so insistently inflicting itself upon the future? Wakes of boats are notoriously transient (though they leave a lot of troubled water). Whitman has out-politicked us again. "Passage" is a *triple entendre*: (1) The literal (fictive) wake-passage of the ferry upon which he purports to cross over while writing the poem; (2) The literary (actual) "passage" (creative process, both finite and infinite) equalling the poem—and unlike the passage of the ferry, this passage will last a long time, maybe forever; (3) The passage (*traditio*), that is, the float-probe, of this poem, written at a particular historical moment (endlessly revised, each revision being an additional historical moment) into the infinite future of American literature. And that is why time, place, and distance avail not. (By now that "prosaic statement" has turned into pure metaphor.)

As Whitman said years later in *Specimen Days* ("My Passion for Ferries"): "What oceanic currents, eddies, underneath—the great tides of humanity also, with ever-shifting movements. Indeed, I have always had a passion for ferries; to me they afford inimitable, streaming, never-failing, living poems." He might have been more explicit. But Whitman never liked being explicit; he wanted us to say it for ourselves. All that motion and energy (as an analogue of his own soul) may well have given him the driving force of the poem. But it was Walt Whitman, poet, who brought it under control, imposed order on it, and placed it on record. (We understand then, do we not, what a constituting metaphor is? What exegetical analysis could not teach is accomplished?) Why, finally, given the float, did Whitman elect a ferry as his constituting metaphor? Ferries go back and forth. So does the poem. Every time the poem is read, the back-and-forth time scheme, together with its metaphorical mate, the mutual writer-reader relationship, is reborn as a new occasion. Every time the poem is read, it disintegrates.

It must be quite clear by now that it is extraordinarily difficult to state precisely just what the constituting metaphor of any particular poem is. The reasons for this difficulty must also be quite clear. The constituting metaphor does not stand for anything else; it *is* itself; being equal to the poem it can only stand for the poem. It was the best way our American poets found to defend themselves against the besetting Anglo-American sin of pseudo-rationalistic reduction, or what Poe called the Didactic Heresy. It was so good a way that Whitman continues to elude most of his critics. It is not quite true, as some have alleged, that he adopts a stance from which symbols proliferate endlessly, with no one to say them yea or nay (indeed, the process is exactly the other way round). More precisely, the principle of constituting metaphor leaves Whitman open to two opposite disasters, the inclusion of minor metaphors insufficiently caused by the constituting metaphor (see a number of the catalogs in "Song of Myself") or the relaxation of the constituting metaphor to the point where its constituted elements will almost inevitably (and this time not the reader's fault) be taken for prose statements, merely chopped up into "lines" (see the more programmatic parts of "Song of the Exposition"). Whitman, like Dante, gladly runs both risks. And often gets away with it. "You have waited, you always wait, you dumb, beautiful ministers." Dumb, beautiful ministers, the American poems have waited, they always wait.

Isolation and identification of constituting metaphor clarify a few curious Whitmanian matters, including some of the more ridiculous statements of the 1855 preface (also untitled). "The United States themselves are essentially the greatest poem" is an almost classic constituting metaphor, not in this instance wrought in a single poem but in a nation's poetry. Taken literally, the phrase is nonsense. Taken figuratively, it is a brilliant constituting metaphor which, as it happens, Whitman and the poets to come have been unable, except partially, to actualize. (But American history is not yet completed.) So I think it goes with most of the presumed allegations of the preface: they are not prose allegations at all but constituting metaphors shaping up. As for metaphor itself, Whitman is lucid enough, if we are. "The expression of the American poet is to be transcendent and new. It is to be indirect and not direct or descriptive or epic." (Whitman moves Poe's constituting metaphor off its too limited narrative base.) Form, form, form, Whitman says, and light, light, light. The emphases are insusceptible of interpretation except as figures organic of the literary situation in which the poet happily finds himself. "He judges not as the judge judges but as the sun falling around a helpless thing": the metaphor is not only witty in itself but the cause that wit is throughout the preface and in the 1855 poems.

Whitman's apparent attacks on "art" do not, on closer inspection, turn out quite that way. "The fluency and ornaments of the finest poems or music or orations . . . are not independent but dependent. . . . Who troubles himself about his ornaments or fluency is lost." That is not a simple-minded assault on ornament and fluency but at attempt to put them in their subordinate place, dependent on the simple trail of idea. Whitman is already in 1855 clearly stating—if we will just listen to him—the principle of constituting metaphor.

"Of ornaments to a work nothing outre can be allowed . . but those ornaments can be allowed that conform to the perfect facts of the open air and that flow out of the nature of the work and come irrepressibly from it and are necessary to the completion of the work." The "nature of the work" is pretty plainly the simple trail of idea, the constituting metaphor, and the ornaments are the faceted, local expressions of it. Therefore Whitman could swear to his art, "I will not be meddlesome." It is the same principle as in sociology or politics: produce great persons, the rest follows. Whitman would produce great metaphors, poems as metaphors, and all the rest would follow. Dependently.

It is along precisely the same line of reasoning that Whitman argues that the poet cannot—that is, he need not, for Whitman was ever the moralist—"moralize or make applications of morals." Neither, according to the ever-religious poet, may he "put God in a poem or system of philosophy as contending against some being or influence."[5] Why should he? In a properly realized poem, morals, and God Himself, attend the constituting metaphors. Whitman's well-nigh incredible equanimity in the face of all conceivable created universes, and the creators of them, directly flows from his habitual manner of dealing with figures of speech. In no other way—not even in metric—was he so modern, radical, and fructifying. "As soon as histories are properly told"—presumably by the poet, or "president of regulation,"—"there is no more need of romances." Whitman's genius was first to have made of history the great romance, and then to have seen that proper history and its constituting metaphors were inextricably fused.

They were fused because the simple, separate person, his national

[5] I suspect he was thinking of *Paradise Lost*, a prime example of how a constituting metaphor can get out of hand, resulting in great confusion between the "good guys" and the "bad guys." Generations of critics have exhausted their inkwells persuading the common reader that Satan is not "really" the hero, and that in the long run God is "right."

culture, world culture, and the infinite nature that cradled them all were fused. In *Democratic Vistas* (1871) Whitman metaphysically insists that "the quality of BEING . . . is the lesson of Nature." Nobody is to "slight" or "overlay" his own "idiocrasy," and yet this idiocrasy, be it of poet or plain man, is also political and cultural and aesthetic: "The spirit and the form are one, and depend far more on association, identity and place, than is supposed." Finally, Whitman writes at length, and eloquently, bringing the whole argument to conclusive climax:

> Observing, rapport, and with intuition, the shows and forms presented by Nature, the sensuous luxuriance, the beautiful in living men and women, the actual play of passions, in history and life—and, above all, from those developments either in Nature or human personality *in which power, (dearest of all to the sense of the artist,) transacts itself*—out of these, and seizing what is in them, the poet, the esthetic worker in any field, by the divine magic of his genius, projects them, their analogies, by curious removes, indirections, in literature and art. (No useless attempt to repeat the material creation, by daguerreotyping the exact likeness by mortal mental means.) This is the image-making faculty, coping with material creation, and rivaling, almost triumphing over it.

Emphasis mine. And Whitman's. Whitman's emphasis on "power, (dearest of all to the sense of the artist,)" transacting itself makes it obvious that by images he means temporal, dynamic forms, namely what I have been calling constituting metaphors. The emphasis on power also makes clear what the typical Whitman constituting metaphor is likely to be, a transfer of energy, managed by analogies, curious removes, and indirections, as, for example, in "Crossing Brooklyn Ferry."

68

The Four Years' War as Pivot

> My book and the war are one.
>
> WHITMAN, "To Thee Old Cause"

AT ONE END of the Whitmanian spectrum we find "Song of Myself," much the longest poem in *Leaves of Grass*, and despite myriad local felicities, many of them uncharacteristically comic, one of the least unified. As I have suggested, its constituting metaphor may never have been found by Whitman, and it has certainly not been found by Whitman's readers except in some vague, over-rationalized, and perhaps even tautological formula like "the self reciprocally in its world." Whitman never again attempted a poem so long or so loosely formed. At the other end of the spectrum we find Whitman's shortest poems, mostly late, nearly all title, or, at best, a title followed by an image ("poemets" he called them). The great poems are those of the middle range, about the poetical length of a short story, like "Crossing Brooklyn Ferry." But clearly, no properly skeptical reader is going to buy my principle of constituting metaphor on the basis of one early example; and meanwhile, there is also a little narrative to be told, the story of how Whitman got from "Out of the Cradle Endlessly Rocking" to "When Lilacs Last in the Dooryard Bloom'd" (apart from "Song of Myself," Whitman's most popular poems). Perhaps the narrative will make more sense if we bracket the tale, glancing first at a poem that postdates the progression by several years, and then comparing that poem with "Crossing Brooklyn Ferry," a poem that predates the progression by several years.

By 1871 Whitman had circumnavigated the globe (backwards) and found himself at the port from which he had set sail, but in somewhat tattered and confused condition. "Passage to India" is

once again a poem of constituting metaphor—all too obviously—
and the metaphor is as usual found in the title. What differentiates
it from the earlier and better poems of constituting metaphor is the
degree of blatancy with which Whitman insists upon explaining,
explicating, and elaborating (not to mention apostrophizing) this
metaphor *seriatim* (engineering, geography, politics, culture, his-
tory, myth, religion, and the Lord knows what all else). Stripped of
this fussy explication, this bland parallelism, and reduced from its
international braggadocio to its basically simple metaphor, "Passage
to India" is immediately recognizable as the same metaphor that
constituted "Crossing Brooklyn Ferry" (just bigger). And worse:
for if "Passage to India" (though it too has local felicities) seems
on first reading to be intellectually more complex than "Crossing
Brooklyn Ferry," it shows itself on second and subsequent readings
to be poetically more crude. The most annoying defect of "Passage
to India" is the way it insistently calls attention to its structure,
whereas the most enchanting beauty of "Crossing Brooklyn Ferry"
is the way it conceals its constituting metaphor, calling attention
instead to its own mysterious being, and to the difficulties of con-
figuring it in a poem.

"Out of the Cradle Endlessly Rocking" (1859 is the date of the
earliest version) is a tougher test case. It is not impossible, however,
to make out its constituting metaphor. The poem was not always
known by that title, and in its peregrinations from title to title, form
to form—"A Child's Reminiscence," "A Word Out of the Sea,"
"Out of the Cradle Endlessly Rocking"—it affords a prime example
of Whitman, long after first composition, long after first publication,
still trying to clarify his constituting metaphor. In the peregrina-
tions we have our clue. Surely there has been too much Puritanical
contention about the respective merits of the several versions of this
poem, and particularly about the title which is also the first line in
the final version. The argument is impossible to adjudicate, since in

revision Whitman marred as much as he mended, and I would glad-
ly have nothing to do with it. Unfortunately, the issue cannot be en-
tirely avoided, since the revisions of the title are closely related to
the poem's constituting metaphor. The "rocked cradle" of 1860,
with the utter finality of that historically-oriented past participle,
prevented Whitman's recognition of his meaning. Changing
"rocked" to "rocking" he suddenly found in the idea of perpetual
process both constituting metaphor and final title; and then for
good measure he again alluded to his newly-shaped metaphor
("endlessly rocking") in the next-to-last line of the poem, not at
all to sentimentalize (a crone is not a sentimental image) but to
seal it tight and make sure it stayed sealed. The poem is an envelope
poem, enveloped in its constituting metaphor, an open-ended prep-
ositional phrase about a situation[6] as "out of the cradle endlessly
rocking."

"Rocked" makes no poetic sense. We are rocked "out" of the
cradle only once, at the precise moment of birth. "Rocked" also
fails poetically to cohere with the key word "death." Whatever may
happen to us at the precise moment of death, "rocked out" is an
execrable metaphor for it, and hopelessly out of tone with the rest
of the poem, indeed with the entire *Leaves of Grass*. More im-
portantly, literal birth is not what Whitman is talking about. He
is talking about the way we lead our lives from moment to moment,
in love and in pain, an endless happening, always being born, al-
ways dying, and how, on special occasions, this process may cul-
minate in a determinant event; in this way, and in this way only, is
the idea of history permissible within the metaphorical context of
the whole poem. Local government can take it the rest of the way
if it likes (but perhaps this poem has been too much explicated
lately?), deducing in ingenious and lovely detail (for the poetical

[6] The "situation" is language, not metaphor, and is discussed at greater
length in the following chapter, pp. 129-134.

materials of the poem are truly lovely, and so is the handling of them) subordinate relationships among boys, birds, poets, wind, moon, sand, stars, waves, and so on. The reader's grip on the poem's constituted unity will not be much advanced. Once he has his hands on the constituting metaphor, he is already free to read it as a poem, and equally free politely to decline the well-meant offices of our endlessly exegetical American critics.

Despite my contention that "A Word Out of the Sea" cannot possibly be the "authorized version" of "Out of the Cradle Endlessly Rocking," because of its failure adequately to understand its constituting metaphor, it remains a remarkable achievement, and just short of ultimate completion. (By ultimate completion I don't necessarily mean the final version; I mean that one or two minor critical revisions concerning the constituting metaphor would have been enough to bring the poem to perfection.) It is far and away the best poem written in the United States up to that time, and most poets would have stopped there. Whitman himself might have stopped there. But suddenly something happened. The war broke over him like a crashing wave, nearly taking him under for good, and when he finally resurfaced he was compelled to rethink his entire enterprise. Now indeed power was transacting itself in a way decidedly *not* "dearest of all to the sense of the artist," and the poet found himself in the thick of the battle, both military and literary.

"My book and the war are one": high time to get to that resounding phrase, that proto-leaf and meta-trope of Whitman's (and our) American poetry. As Whitman wrote in the Centennial preface of 1876: "the whole book, indeed, revolves around that four years' war, which, as I was in the midst of it, becomes, in 'Drum-Taps,' pivotal to the rest entire." The most conspicuous pivot of *Drum-Taps* (1865-66) is "Song of the Banner at Daybreak," one of the most self-conscious poems Whitman ever wrote, and wonderfully revealing of his long-range ambitions and problems. It is also—another of its revelations—imperfectly realized. Whitman has relapsed to his old titling habits. "Song of the Banner at Daybreak" has some of that attributive quality of the 1856 titles. The title sounds temporary, as if Whitman hadn't yet thought of the real one. (And he never did.) The poem is also divided into sections, which are voices, somewhat as in the earlier versions of "Out of the Cradle Endlessly Rocking," but this time Whitman let them stand, declining to reconcile the war of words and noises, which include speeches by banner and pennant, going one or more better the talking birds and surf of "The Raven" and "Out of the Cradle Endlessly Rocking." Such a poem would naturally have great difficulty locating and establishing its constituting metaphor. Perhaps the metaphor was never found—not within the limits of the poem, anyway, though very possibly within the limits of *Leaves of Grass* and of American poetry—and Whitman left the poem unfinished as a sort of central preface. It is still Whitman's best statement of the pivotal fact of his poetic career—a fact he was forever asserting, for all the good it did him—that the Civil War, standing for all democratic conflict, and the collapse of all "Union" (that ever-elusive constituting metaphor), was to the body politic what the thought of death is to the citizen, that which brings forth the quality of the soul. Finally, "Song of the Banner at Daybreak" is the central point of our narrative, the bridge from "Out of the Cradle Endlessly Rocking" to "When Lilacs Last in the Dooryard Bloom'd." The war poem frequently glances backward to the language poem and it points forward to the assassination poem rather more than we would expect a poem to point to a poem not yet written about a historical calamity that had not yet occurred.

"Song of the Banner at Daybreak" is Whitman's effort to blast his way out of "Out of the Cradle Endlessly Rocking" (or to give it its 1860 title once more, and pertinently, "A Word Out of the

Sea"). It begins with a call for "a new song, a free song," which will transcend "Words! book-words!" ("what are you?"), including, presumably, the book-word "death," which had so handsomely brought to birth Whitman's finest poem to date. Now he wants to "put in life," even if it wrecks the poem, and so the banner speaks, and a pennant, and a child, and the child's fearful Philistine father, and the poet speaks, "as one carrying a symbol and menace far into the future." (This line was not in the original text. Its parenthetical addition suggests Whitman's growing apprehension of the broader implications of his theme.) Banner and pennant speak best—as the Child says, "O father it is alive—it is full of people—it has children,/ O now it seems to me it is talking to its children,/ I hear it —it talks to me"—and as ever the poet listens and translates, ultimately committing himself to a poetry that goes way beyond all American poetry:

Fusing and holding, claiming, devouring the whole,
No more with tender lip, nor musical labial sound,
But out of the night emerging for good, our voice persuasive
    no more,
Croaking like crows here in the wind.

The banner obviously speaks for Whitman, ostensibly contending for the need to take into full poetic account the actual horrors of the war. (But what is meant by "our voice persuasive no more"? an end to hortatory poetry? if so, too bad the admonition wasn't followed.) It may include also the echo of the voice of Poe croaking in the wind ("crows" is plural) on his way to the bust of Pallas ("passions of demons [and] . . . premature death" are among the Father's phobias), for the newly-sophisticated Whitman was already on the way to realizing—as spelled out in *Democratic Vistas*—that the achievement of a national literature, and even of a nation, involved a more desperate struggle than the campaign presently being fought out over the nation's political existence.

Now, as the *Poet* says, "My theme is clear at last." This banner ("leading the day with stars brought from the night!") and this pennant ("O you up there! . . . where you undulate like a snake hissing") are more than common military rhetoric. (Whitman had also written a few poems of that sort.) Beyond Union, democracy, America, "out of reach, an idea only," is the nameless reality of which these are only historical instances, the nameless atmosphere that is the sustenance of this poem, and of all poems. To it war-torn Whitman rededicates himself (he had opened the very first *Leaves of Grass* in 1855 with an invocation to fresh air): henceforth, "I sing you only,/ Flapping up there in the wind." War had become the constituting metaphor—almost as constituent as "leaves," and perhaps more so—of his poetic life. "Song of the Banner at Daybreak" shows us the process by which the metaphor was won, and why it was worth fighting for; but it just barely hints the full significance of the victory; that was to come later, slowly, and imperfectly.

"*Power,*" Whitman said laconically in *Specimen Days* ("A Two Hours' Ice-Sail"), "so important in poetry and war." He offers no explanation of what sounds like a virtual equivalence—understandable only if we happen to recur to the phrase about power transacting itself; but still not very clear. Whitman never was very clear on the subject, though he improved with time. In 1881 he transferred to *Drum-Taps* "Adieu to a Soldier," in which we find these lines:

> Adieu dear comrade,
> Your mission is fulfill'd—but I, more warlike,
> Myself and this contentious soul of mine,
> Still on our own campaigning bound . . .
> To fiercer, weightier battles give expression.

In his introductory "Inscriptions," Whitman was even more contentious on the subject, but not much more specific. In "As I Ponder'd in Silence," a rather Dante-like old "Phantom" (certainly he is medieval and austere enough) charges Whitman:

> With finger pointing to many immortal songs,
> And menacing voice, *What singest thou?* it said,
> *Know'st thou not there is but one theme*
> >   *for ever-enduring bards?*
> *And that is the theme of War, the fortune of battles,*
> *The making of perfect soldiers.*

To which Whitman haughtily replies:

> *Be it so*, then I answer'd,
> *I too haughty Shade also sing war, and a longer*
> >   *and greater one than any,*
> *Waged in my book with varying fortune, with flight,*
> >   *advance and retreat, victory deferr'd and wavering,*
> *(Yet methinks certain, or as good as certain, at the last,)*
> >   *the field the world,*
> *For life and death, for the Body and for*
> >   *the eternal Soul,*
> *Lo, I too am come, chanting the chant of battles,*
> *I above all promote brave soldiers.*

Or in "Shut Not Your Doors" (once a *Drum-Taps* poem), "Forth from the war emerging, a book I have made,/ The words of my book nothing, the drift of it every thing."

Words and war and books and drift. When a poet insists on stating his case so broadly, he requires interpretation. Fortunately, the interpretation can be simple and brief. The facts are all before us: (1) Whitman loosely and variously used the constituting metaphor of war for any struggle whatsoever, including *Leaves of Grass*; (2) *Leaves of Grass* was Whitman's life-long struggle simultaneously and reciprocally to create an American poetry and the American people; (3) the war metaphor was a natural for Whitman. America was baptized in blood, just as much as in the written Constitution or the earlier Declaration, and then later confirmed in its own hemorrhage. The first war was a defiant onslaught against mother, the second war an act of adolescent self-destruction. Both wars are analogized, reflected, and continued down to the present day in the American poets' perpetual struggle to create an American poetry against English odds and their own internal divisions. Once again we move from poetry to politics and back again; for war, after all, is nothing more than politics driven to the thin edge of insanity.

The narrative ends with "When Lilacs Last in the Dooryard Bloom'd," Whitman's elegy for President Lincoln, the war-winning, peace-loving president theatrically assassinated after the conclusion of the war. That nasty irony obviously hit Whitman even harder than the fratricidal war. Here was no longer process, nor even inimical struggle, but tragic and irremediable finality. As in "Out of the Cradle Endlessly Rocking," the constituting metaphor is a prepositional phrase ordained in the title and in the first line, but the two titles radically differ in their grammar, "rocking" vs "bloom'd." For the poem of particular historical occasion, Whitman properly shifted to past tense. *Explication de texte* has had its customary field day with Whitman's triune symbolism of lilac and star and thrush. Because of their simple and mechanical nature, these things obtrude; their true significance is in their being accidents of the real presence of the poem, the antithesis between locations or fixed objects (such as the three symbols) and the people who travel through them. Except for the star, which sets, the symbols go nowhere; they do not develop; that is precisely their point. Only Lincoln and Whitman move, and one of them is dead. The journey of the dead man's coffin Westward and backward is repeatedly contrasted with the insouciant stability of the American landscape through which the funeral train grinds its way. As the coffin goes by, Whitman, here stationary, offers his sprig of lilac, a gesture of deliberate futility, which then engenders further futilities: "O how shall I warble myself for the dead one there I loved?" and "O what shall I hang on the chamber walls . . . To adorn the burial-house?" What, indeed, except this recalcitrant poem that will apparently not be written? ("Sing on there in the swamp . . . I hear, I come presently." But is very slow getting around to it.) How shall I warble, what shall I hang: the questions are dead ends except as the poem stubbornly proceeds against the obstacles of which it is deliberately composed. (You can't really write a poem about an assassinated president, you have to take it by analogies, curious removes, and indirections.) The poem is about blockage and headway.

The blockage ends only with Whitman "fled forth to the hiding receiving night that talks not"—the remark is virtually the description of his best metaphorical practice—where finally the voice of his spirit tallies the song of the bird. It is, of course, as in "Out of the Cradle Endlessly Rocking," but with differences appropriate to the different intentions of the two poems, a "Song of the bleeding throat,/ Death's outlet song of life, (for well dear brother I know,/ If thou wast not granted to sing thou would'st surely die.)" And Whitman is, of course, not just any run-of-the-mill American poet: "the singer so shy to the rest receiv'd me." As a result of the tally, Whitman's uninspired catalog landscapes, which closely resemble the landscapes in many earlier Whitman poems, are metamorphosed into "long panoramas of visions," a vastly different affair, realistic versions of reality, sights and sounds of the Four Years' War, corpses, "myriads of them,/ And the white skeletons of young men," and the suffering, helpless survivors. From such depths of pain the poem finally rises through a string of present participles to a deliberate relinquishment of its symbols, "yet each to keep and all." What Whitman mostly kept was his ruined comrades, most of them young enough to be his own sons, "the dead I loved so well," among whom the great president finally takes his appropriately humble place.

The constituting metaphor of the poem is the prepositional phrase, "when lilacs last in the dooryard bloom'd" with its curious death-life emphasis on "bloom'd" ("fresh as the morning, thus would I chant a song for you O sane and sacred death"), and with its curious preposition "when." When I last wrote a poem, a particular poem, when this particular poem bloomed, "spotting the grey debris": the constituting metaphor does not predicate, it points; here it points to the word where Whitman has impounded the historical and meta-physical mysteries of pastness in the grammatical mystery of "when."[7] Lilacs do not bloom all the time, but spring comes around every year. Not, however, the spring of 1865. That spring is more than a century behind us, and every year it retreats a little further. Whitman knew it would, and shaped his metaphor accordingly.[8] Not only the assassination and the elegy receded; Whitman receded (in 1873 he suffered a paralytic stroke probably induced by his war-time work as wound-dresser in the military hospitals of Washington). He may have had a premonition. "As my soul in its trouble dissatisfied sank, as where you sad orb"—"O powerful western fallen star!"—"Concluded, dropt in the night, and was gone." Early American poetry—so largely the invention of a single man—was over.

---

[7] There is also great mystery about the word "last." Did Whitman merely mean his most recent poem? Or did he guess that he was at a breaking-point in his career?

[8] "I suppose it is hardly necessary to tell you," he wrote much later, "that I have *pitched* and *keyed* my pieces more with reference to fifty years hence, & how they will stand mellowed and toned *then*—than to pleasing & tickling the immediate impressions of the present hour" (letter of 28 July 1874 to Rudolf Schmidt).

The Waste Land and the *Cantos*

Shall two know the same in their knowing?
 You who dare Persephone's threshold,
 Beloved, do not fall apart in my hands.

POUND, 93 *de los cantares*

As in Whitman, the major modern American poems are organized by a constituting metaphor, which usually appears in the title, and which establishes an area of figurative discourse within which a sometimes quite astonishing diversity of material can be brought to poetic life. (And sometimes not. These poems are even more ambitious than Whitman's, and often fall apart in the poet's—or reader's—hands.) Partly because the poems are so ambitious, they are frequently misread, and it is therefore fairly common to find them in company with prose explanations. (Not necessarily in public. As in the case of Hart Crane's *The Bridge*, the "explanation" may take the form of an intensive private correspondence.) Even Whitman felt it necessary to indulge a good deal of journalistic hinting and pointing for "Out of the Cradle Endlessly Rocking" ("A Child's Reminiscence" in its first newspaper appearance). "The curious warble . . . well-enveloped, and eluding definition. . . . The piece will bear reading many times—perhaps, indeed, only comes forth, as from recesses, by many repetitions." Perhaps that can stand as the motto for the behavior of the constituting metaphor in general.

In an equally mystifying yet suggestive way Eliot hints with his title and with the introduction to his notes the meaning of his major poem, *The Waste Land* (1922), that is to say, its constituting metaphor. Title first. It conspicuously hovers between death and life. "Waste," for example, hovers between "desert" and "good land gone to waste, or devastated," and it also contains connotations of useless

80

expenditure, garbage, or excrementa. (And so much more.)[9] Syntactically, the word "waste" hovers between adjective and past participle. It is impossible to keep the time element from creeping in, and therefore the poem is not merely about a static condition, but about the etiology, pathology, and therapy of deserts, together with some of their attendant implications (garbage, for example, linguistic, sexual, cultural, and spiritual). "The river bears no empty bottles, sandwich papers,/ Silk handkerchiefs, cardboard boxes, cigarette ends/ Or other testimony of summer nights." Maybe, but only because in these particular lines it isn't summer.

Introduction to the notes. "Not only the title, but the plan and a good deal of the incidental symbolism of the poem were suggested by Miss Jessie L. Weston's book on the Grail legend: *From Ritual to Romance* (Cambridge). Indeed, so deeply am I indebted, Miss Weston's book will elucidate the difficulties of the poem much better than my notes can do; and I recommend it (apart from the great interest of the book itself) to any who think such elucidation of the poem worth the trouble." When Old Possum plays that way, what are we practical cats to do? Taken at face value, Eliot's statement is leg-pull or goose-chase: reference to Jessie L. Weston can only carry us away from the poem, not into it. (Eliot cunningly covers himself on this point by offering only "such" elucidation as "such" reference is capable of providing. A whole generation of critics thought he was offering them catnip, and rolled in it.) "Not only the title, but the plan and a good deal of the incidental symbolism of the poem. . . ." This is still the metaphorical world of Poe and Whitman. The title and plan are of course the constituting metaphor or under-current, and the incidental symbols are the localized facets of it. (And aside from meters and voices, what else is there?)

[9] There is a good deal of poetic mileage to be got from the *OED* entry for "waste," including some unexpected, because obsolete, meanings concerned with writing and printing. I have an uncanny sense that I am not the first reader who has passed this way.

Then why all this devious palaver about Miss Weston? Perhaps it is not in the long run so much the vegetative content of Miss Weston's mythological researches that concerns us poetically as it is her title. Anyone who looks *at* that title—instead of through or past it to the book it refers to—will soon enough see that it is the title itself that provides Eliot a secondary constituting metaphor, closely in tandem with (practically identical with) his primary constituting metaphor of "waste land." When we actually get to the poem, we find it in fact shaped by a movement "from ritual to romance," a haltingly redemptive journey from meaningless social manners to what looks like at least a putative burgeoning of eros. In "I. The Burial of the Dead" we find this kind of poetry (empty ritual):

> Summer surprised us, coming over the Starnbergersee
> With a shower of rain; we stopped in the colonnade,
> And went on in sunlight, into the Hofgarten,
> And drank coffee, and talked for an hour.
> Bin gar keine Russin, stamm' aus Litauen, echt deutsch.
> And when we were children, staying at the archduke's
> My cousin's . . .

This is all very well, but what did they talk about, and why the senseless name-drop? On and on and on it goes through Madame Sosostris and other piles of garbage. At the other end of the poem, in "V. What the Thunder Said," just a few lines before the poem breaks toward hysteria and begins to run like a movie film out of control ("London Bridge is falling down falling down falling down"), we find poetry like this (happy and dignified foreplay):

> The boat responded
> Gaily, to the hand expert with sail and oar
> The sea was calm, your heart would have responded
> Gaily, when invited, beating obedient
> To controlling hands.

That may not be Tristan and Isolde, but it's a long step up the unlit stairs from the young man carbuncular. Maybe the waste land is breaking up and coming to life again. For those who can read the poem, it is.[10]

With Ezra Pound's *Cantos*, we must be altogether more wary and speculative. It is still a work in progress, and it may never be completed. (Pound was born in 1885.)[11] We are not entirely sure whether the *Cantos* (or *The Cantos*) is the true and final title of the poem. Two cantos (72 and 73) are missing, and they might contain clues to the whole. (On the other hand, they may just as well have been withheld as too scurrilous for present publication. Much more likely, they represent an interruption in Pound's work on the American history sequence, caused by his incarceration at Pisa at the end of the Second World War.) It is always an open possibility that the poem has no constituting metaphor at all. But that is not how the poem sounds to even the beginning reader. Whatever else Pound has or does not have—for example, the ability always to communicate clearly—he has and always has had authority and control. It is a perilous and arrogant leap of critical judgment to assume that we confront in the *Cantos* the product of a magpie mind.

On the other hand, it is just as perilous to play the game of Inside Dopester. Here is what once resulted from a conversation between Pound and Yeats:

> He [Pound] explains that it [that immense poem] will, when the hundredth canto is finished, display a structure like that of a Bach Fugue. There will be no plot, no chronicle of events, no

[10] In this chapter I restrict myself to *The Waste Land*, as Eliot's only major poem demonstrably built on constituting metaphor. I can locate no constituting metaphor in "Ash Wednesday," which appears to take the form of a prayer or meditation. *Four Quartets* openly proclaims itself to be a suite of poems and passages in musical counterpoint.

[11] Since I wrote this, Pound has died, and it is obvious that the *Cantos* will never be finished. Still, it seems best to let my original remarks stand, but with a slightly different emphasis on the words "wary" and "speculative."

logic of discourse, but two themes, the Descent into Hades from Homer, a Metamorphosis from Ovid, and, mixed with these, mediaeval or modern historical characters. . . . He has scribbled on the back of an envelope certain sets of letters that represent emotions or archetypal events—I cannot find any adequate definition —A B C D and then J K L M, and then each set of letters repeated, and then A B C D inverted and this repeated, and then a new element X Y Z, then certain letters that never recur, and then all sorts of combinations of X Y Z and J K L M and A B C D and D C B A, and all set whirling together.   (*A Vision*)

Contrapasso for writing on the backs of envelopes and entrusting them to Celtic poets. "God damn Yeats' bloody paragraph," Pound exploded in a letter. "Done more to prevent people reading Cantos for what is *on the page* than any other one smoke screen" (letter of February 1939). And in another letter: "If Yeats knew a fugue from a frog, he might have transmitted what I told him in some way that would have helped rather than obfuscated *his* readers. Mah!!!" (letter of April 1937).

Other readers have had their plausible but conflicting says about the constituting metaphor of the *Cantos*, usually relying upon some "central" passage in the poem or in Pound's prolific prose. Pound's "*forma*," his "immortal *concetto*," is naturally the rose pattern driven into the iron-filings. Didn't Pound practically say so in that passage I quoted in the opening paragraph of this chapter? But what is naturally central to Reader One is just as naturally incidental to Reader Two. The constituting metaphor, says Reader Two, is of course the perennial war between usury and the man who wants to do a good job. (And he too has a scriptural text in hand. Everybody does.) Reader Three puts his chips on metamorphoses and repeats in history, and, after re-examination, finds Yeats' explanations not altogether mad. Reader Four is convinced that the *Cantos* is a modern *Odyssey* (as canto 1 suggests), a sort of poetic parallel to Joyce's *Ulysses*, but somehow out of hand. Reader Five immediately counters that, in general, Pound's epic of modern man in search of his soul's tradition more nearly resembles the *Aeneid*. But to Reader Six all this is fuss and feathers: the whole performance smacks mainly of intellectual and literary autobiography, and he asks of the poem no further unity than that of an endless diary and journal (brilliantly and sporadically "poetic"). Reader Seven, who has a sharp eye, but is a bad guesser, notices that the title of the poem is plural—simply "the songs"—and is content to drop the matter there.

Other poet-friends besides Yeats have had a try at the *Cantos*. The most stimulating, although somewhat confused try, is perhaps William Carlos Williams' 1935 review. His first attempt at the poem is as follows: "That all men are contemporaries, in whatever time they live or have lived, whose minds (including the body and its acts) have lifted them above the sordidness of a grabbing world—would seem to be the general theme of the *Cantos*." That is a bit vague and nonhistorical to be the final answer, and indeed a couple of paragraphs later Williams has noticeably shifted emphasis: "Love versus usury, the living hell-stink of today. . . ." But that cannot possibly be the answer, since most of the *Cantos* concerns the past. Still a couple of paragraphs later Williams is on another kick, though still in the present tense and carelessly overlooking the fact that Dante's *Commedia* comes in three parts (a fact to which Pound frequently alludes): "The *Cantos* should become an Index of the Damned and the Damnable, the anatomized *Inferno* of our lives today." Be that as it may, the *Cantos* is unarguably the inferno of modern American criticism.

For all the obvious vagueness and uncertainty—it must be remembered that Williams was writing early in the day, and that the greatest bulk of the Dante material turns up in the later cantos—I think Williams was a remarkably good guesser. Temporary or not,

Pound's title has been around a long time, and it pretty plainly invites us to consider the *Cantos* in a Dantean light.[12] And when we do, what we find is this. The *Cantos*—*among other things*—is a secularized and re-paganized version of the *Commedia* (for Pound was no lover of Aquinas, Christianity, Judaism, or Virgil). The secularization occurs through Pound's quixotic attempt to isolate Dante from his context, to extract his essence ("detach Dantescan light" from the Middle Ages is one of Pound's most revealing self-admonitions). The re-paganization occurs through Pound's marriage, or at least juxtaposition, of the *Commedia* with the *Odyssey* and other Greek texts (as Pound is fond of pointing out, Dante couldn't read Greek). The chief difference (for the *Cantos-Commedia* analogue involves nearly as much contrast as comparison) is that Dante is eschatological, and pilgrim-Dante travels toward a fixed if ineffable point, whereas Pound is historical, and pilgrim-Pound (or whatever other name one chooses to attach to this "factive" personality) travels through a history that is itself in motion through time, either toward or away from the light. It is almost too obvious for comment that Pound does not take up Dante's three states of being in order but scatters and mixes them throughout, in the best modern way. "By no means an orderly Dantescan rising," as Pound says in one of his loveliest fusions of Dante and Homer, "but as the winds veer/ ... as the winds veer and the raft is driven" (canto 74).

Pound's poetic handling of his constituting metaphor is far more complicated, and apparently more nominalistic, than any other constituting metaphor hitherto encountered. There is, of course, the constant invitation to contrast and compare; but within that general framework there is great variety of local application. There are fairly obvious, though not exact, "imitations" of Dante, as in the Hell cantos (cantos 14-15). But Pound is much more likely to scat-

[12] What follows is a brief résumé of the central argument of my article "Dante and Pound's *Cantos*," *Journal of Modern Literature*, I (First Issue 1970), 75-87.

ter brief allusions to the *Commedia* (and other writings of Dante) as they come to mind or are magnetized to his matter. Many of these allusions appear to function analogously as reminders of what once occurred in Dante and is now occurring in Pound; that is, these allusions not only refer backward to the *Commedia* but they serve as structural signposts in the ongoing *Cantos*. This kind of allusion tends to be fairly open and aboveboard (if it were not, its function would be thwarted), as, for example, in canto 23, "Precisely, the selv' oscura," or in canto 74, "we who have passed over Lethe." Signposts is precisely the word for them: they tell us where we now are. (In less obvious instances Pound often cites the canto in Dante to which he refers.)

Another of Pound's favorite metaphorical techniques—I am of course talking now about the localized facets of the constituting metaphor, not the constituting metaphor itself—is the conjunction of two or more Dantean passages in order to create a new poetic synthesis, sometimes ironic, sometimes lyric:

> And from far
> > il tremolar della marina . . .
> > "fui chiamat'
> > > e qui refulgo"   (canto 92)

First the famous showpiece of Dantean technique (*Purgatorio*, I, 117; "the trembling of the sea"), and then Pound's great love and heroine, Cunizza, speaking in *Paradiso*, IX, 32 ("I was called, and here I shine"). The juncture of passages blends two diverse but equally tremulous lyric epiphanies into a new motion definable only by its inexpressible union of light waves drawing purgatory into paradise and nature into man. Finally there are concentrations of Dante in particular cantos, large, knotted clusters or clumps of allusion, which may occupy a minority of the lines, but overwhelmingly. Such clusters are far too complex for analysis here. The reader who wants to play amateur Dantista can get a run for his money in canto 93. (For good measure, he might take it in context with the conspicuous efflorescence of Dantean material in cantos 90-92 and cantos 94-99.)

But what does this all add up to? Fairly simple, I think, in general outline, however difficult in the interpretation of detail. For our time and situation, Dante offers more light than any other single man. Detaching that light from its accidentals, we can begin to see how recurrently through history we have all gone to hell in a handbasket, got saved, and fallen away. Through literary and economic knowledge and good works, we can get saved again, even in the twentieth century. If Pound can resurrect the entire historical past— he doesn't do so literally, but that's the impression he tries to give— he can resurrect us too. Some readers will buy all of Pound's message, even the stupid and revolting anti-Semitism; other readers will buy most of it, but make their own private subtractions; other readers will buy selected parts (the sorts that make their way into anthologies); while still other readers will reject it out of hand (usually without a reading). What can't be rejected or overlooked is the enormity of Pound's heave. Unless one counts *Leaves of Grass* as a single work, the *Cantos* is the most ambitious poem in American history.

The Genesis of Hart Crane's *The Bridge*

One arc synoptic of all tides below

CRANE, *The Bridge*

NATURALLY every poet thinks that his own great poem is the most ambitious poem in American history. What all American poets seem to agree on is the necessity for explanation and, with poets less self-assured than Pound, justification. Hart Crane's *The Bridge* had to be endlessly explained to friends, and of course it had to be justified to his financial benefactor Otto Kahn. Crane's last surviving letter to Kahn (12 September 1927) sets the problem:

What I am really handling, you see, is the Myth of America. Thousands of strands have had to be searched for, sorted and interwoven. In a sense I have had to do a great deal of pioneering myself. It has taken a great deal of energy—which has not been so difficult to summon as the necessary patience to wait, simply wait much of the time—until my instincts assured me that I had assembled my materials in proper order for a final welding into their natural form. For each section of the entire poem has presented its own unique problem of form, not alone in relation to the materials embodied within its separate confines, but also in relation to the other parts, *in series*, of the major design of the entire poem. Each is a separate canvas, as it were, yet none yields its entire significance when seen apart from the others. One might take the Sistine Chapel as an analogy. . . . I am really writing an epic of the modern consciousness, and indescribably complicated factors have to be resolved and blended. . . . The range of *The Bridge* has been called colossal by more than one critic who has seen the ms. And though I have found the subject to be vaster than I had at first realized, I am still highly confident of its final articulation into a continuous and eloquent span.

The letter is much longer, of course, but I have deliberately cut Crane off at the critical point where in his epistolary prose he picks up his own title and constituting metaphor as a metaphor for the successful formal completion of his poem. The letter is full of insecure pomposity, but Crane does finally come to the point: the point of *The Bridge*, its final articulation and its only possible span, is contained in the title, the constituting metaphor, the enabling act toward which Crane was so tortuously working his way. The job for criticism is to read the poem in the light of this metaphor and title, that is, to take hold of the poem from the angle of "bridgeness" in all its poetically substantiated states, and to make sense of it, or, alternatively, to determine that no federal sense can be made. (The job is no different than for "Out of the Cradle Endlessly Rocking," *The Waste Land*, or any other poem of constituting metaphor.)

Because Crane wrote so many letters about it, *The Bridge* is the best-documented example we have of at least one way in which a poem of constituting metaphor may come into being. The most important revelation is the first (which is also the last): Crane commenced with a title and a metaphor, and little else. On 6 February 1923 he wrote as much to Allen Tate and Gorham Munson. To Tate: "I'm already started on a new poem, *The Bridge*, which continues the tendencies that are evident in 'Faustus and Helen,' but it's too vague and nebulous yet to talk about." To Munson: "I am ruminating on a new longish poem under the title of *The Bridge* which carries on further the tendencies manifest in 'F and H.' It will be exceedingly difficult to accomplish it as I see it now, so much time will be wasted in thinking about it." That was a candid and accurate prophecy. Then on 20 February he wrote an unknown correspondent: "I'm on a synthesis of America and its structural identity now, called *The Bridge*." The introduction of America as a synthesis and a structural identity looks like a great advance, but is probably not; given Crane's propensities, these themes must have been impounded in his first instinctual poetic move, his titling; even in this letter, the key sentence ends with the title. Crane is virtually in his initial position still: America is a synthesis and a structural identity figured by his constituting metaphor and title, but he does not know what poetic matter might be thereby constituted. The whole argument has a strongly circular quality.

One crucial difficulty soon identified itself. *The Bridge* was, or was to become, the "continuous and eloquent span" between the American past (Crane was no historian) and the American future (about which Crane knew no more than Calvin Coolidge). Still Crane pursued his elusive metaphor. Two days earlier than the letter in which he briefly announced that America was a synthesis, he tried to elucidate his intention, somewhat hysterically, to Munson (18 February 1923):

It is just beginning to take the least outline,—and the more outline the conception of the thing takes,—the more its final difficulties appal me. All this preliminary thought has to result, of course, in some channel forms or mould into which I throw myself at white heat. Very roughly, it concerns a mystical synthesis of "America." History and fact, location, etc., all have to be transfigured into abstract form that would almost function independently of its subject matter. [The Wallace Stevens fallacy.] The initial impulses of "our people" will have to be gathered up toward the climax of the bridge, symbol of our constructive future, our unique identity, in which is included also our scientific hopes and achievements of the future. The mystic portent of all this is already flocking through my mind . . . but the actual statement of the thing, the marshalling of the forces, will take me months, at best; and I may have to give it up entirely before that; it may be too impossible an ambition. But if I do succeed, such a waving of banners, such ascent of towers, such dancing, etc., will never before have been put down on paper! The form will be symphonic.

Even with all this massive correspondence, we do not really know, as the poet knows, how *The Bridge* came into being, that is to say, we do not have the inside intuitive poetic knowledge of what Crane felt when writing these letters, and, more importantly, how he felt between the letters, when he was writing trial drafts or merely thinking about his problem. All we have are external pointers. But what they point to is extraordinarily valuable: it is highly probable that *The Bridge* is a classic case of how poems of constituting metaphor enter the world. Sometimes the title comes first (as in Crane) sometimes last (as in some Whitman poems). What all these poems have in common is a powerful poetic intuition, felt as a metaphorical form that will yield the structure of the poem as soon as the metaphorical import of the intuition can be determined.

"Terrific threshold of the prophet's pledge," as the poem says. Crane was now on the threshold, and he would stay there a long time, waiting and suffering. Clearly uncertain how to proceed, Crane next tried the Poe game (he need not have had Poe consciously in mind, of course): he wrote the *dénouement* first, and many times. The earliest inkling we have of this is a letter to Alfred Stieglitz of 25 August 1923: "I've been in such despair about this latter [*The Bridge*] for some time!—not seeing my way to introduce it in the way I want (the end and climax, what you have seen, is all that's done so far)." Crane had good reason to use as the epigraph for *The Bridge* a quotation from the Book of Job: "From going to and fro in the earth, and from walking up and down in it." *Two and a half years* after the letter to Stieglitz, Crane had neither much changed nor substantially advanced his position. To Waldo Frank on 18 January 1926: "I am not through working on it yet, but I thought you might care to see this last part of *The Bridge*, oddly enough emergent first." What he sent was far, far, far from the final version, though its general outline was pretty well firmed up. (For present purposes, the most telling phrase, later deleted, is the following attributive metaphor of the bridge that was the poem: "synoptic foliating dome.") In March the same story and the same despair-elation ambivalence, understandable enough in view of what a constituting metaphor demands and promises, especially this one; it is not surprising that the ambivalence continues into the final version of the text, which in many aspects is a prayer, and more precisely a prayer that this particular poem may be accomplished ("And of the curveship lend a myth to God"). To Charlotte and Richard Rychtarik on 2 March 1926: "The finale . . . is just about completed—but the antecedent sections will take me at least a year yet. At times the project seems hopeless, horribly so; and then suddenly something happens inside one, and the theme and the substance of the conception seem brilliantly real, more so than ever! At least, *at worst*, the poem will be a *huge* failure!" It is of course neither, but rather a brilliantly concatenated series of lyric poems of uneven quality, which clearly relate to each other but never entirely coalesce.

Reporting in to Otto Kahn on 18 March Crane presents a somewhat more confident picture. "It concludes at midnight—at the center of Brooklyn Bridge. Strangely enough that final section of the poem has been the first to be completed,—yet there's a logic to it, after all; it is the mystic consummation toward which all the other sections of the poem converge. Their contents are implicit in its summary." For "mystic" read "metaphorical." And then a couple of paragraphs later Crane makes a statement bringing news of a progress we have not yet heard about. (Naturally the statement may be more wish-fulfillment than literal fact.) "As I said, I have thus far completed only the final section,—about one hundred lines. I am now going straight through from the beginning." Whether or not Crane was running a little ahead of himself in his letter to Kahn, he was surely on the verge of a great discovery, though it emerged only after another half-year of alternating pain and desire. On 5 April he wrote Gorham Munson that his poetic powers were "frozen," despite the fact that "in so many ways I know what I WANT to do." But Crane clearly did not know what he wanted to do—why else should he peevishly capitalize the word, and describe himself as droning about, "reading, eating and sleeping?" And Crane had still to descend to a lower circle before he began his real progress. Around June (20 June 1926 letter to Waldo Frank) his constituting metaphor collapsed. The reason for the collapse is plain. Crane had lost his confidence in the American present and future, and therefore his constituting metaphor contradicted what he really felt. The issue is so crucial that we had better hear him out on it:

> Emotionally I should like to write *The Bridge*; intellectually judged the whole theme and project seems more and more absurd. . . . I had what I thought were authentic materials . . . [but] these "materials" were valid to me to the extent that I presumed them to be (articulate or not) at least organic and active factors in the experience and perceptions of our common race, time and belief. The very idea of a bridge, of course, is a form peculiarly dependent on such spiritual convictions. It is an act of faith besides being a communication. The symbols of reality necessary to articulate the span—may not exist where you expected them, however. By which I mean that however great their subjective significance to me is concerned—these forms, materials, dynamics are simply non-existent in the world. I may amuse and delight and flatter myself as much as I please—but I am only evading a recognition and playing Don Quixote in an immorally conscious way. . . . The bridge as a symbol today has no significance.

And then rather pathetically added: "If only America were half as worthy today to be spoken of as Whitman spoke of it fifty years ago there might be something for me to say."

That looks like a total collapse, but in fact it proved otherwise; it was only the collapse, or, as is evident in the final poem, the diminution of Crane's past-future metaphor. He was now free to develop the matter in a somewhat different and more promising direction. To Waldo Frank on 3 August 1926, exultingly: "I feel as though I were dancing on dynamite these days—so absolute and elaborated has become the conception. All sections moving forward now at once! I didn't realize that a bridge is begun from the two ends at once." This was Crane's great revelation. His constituting metaphor was now transformed from a mystical synthesis of past-future America to a reflexive analogue of the very act of the poem in the process of building itself toward its metaphorical span. Spanning the beginning and end of a poem, rather than the backward glances and democratic vistas of the nation, *The Bridge* became poetically possible. *The Bridge* had quite simply become for Crane what Whitman had hoped *Leaves of Grass* would be for himself, "my definitive *carte visite* to the coming generations of the New World" ("A Backward Glance O'er Travel'd Roads").

Things continued to go well. On 12 August Crane wrote Frank: "The accumulation of impressions and concepts gathered the last several years and constantly repressed by immediate circumstances [and, as we have seen, by false leads] are having a chance to function, I believe. And nothing but this large form would hold them without the violences that mar so much of my previous, more casual work. *The Bridge* is already longer than *The Wasteland*,—and it's only about half done." Apparently Crane had not heard about Pound's famous congratulations to Eliot for having written the longest poem in the English language. A week later (19 August) Crane wrote Frank again: "I'm glad to know that *The Bridge* is fulfilling your utmost intuitions; for an intuition it undoubtedly was." Undoubtedly; as I have been piling up all this evidence to demonstrate.

Four years later *The Bridge* was completed, and Crane was defending its doubtful unity (letter of 22 April 1930) to Herbert Weinstock: "It is pertinent to suggest, I think, that with more time and familiarity with *The Bridge* you will come to envisage it more as one poem with a clearer and more integrated unity and development than was at first evident. At least if my own experience in reading and re-reading Eliot's *Wasteland* has any relation to the circumstances this *may* be found to be the case. It took me nearly five years, with innumerable readings to convince myself of the essential unity of that poem. And *The Bridge* is at least as complicated in its structure and inferences as *The Wasteland*—perhaps more so." The emphasis on "may" is suggestive. But Crane at least appeared to be on the whole satisfied with the results of his long agony. To Allen Tate on 13 July 1930 he very peacefully wrote more or less what he had first announced to Tate and Munson seven years earlier: "I shall be humbly grateful if *The Bridge* can fulfil simply the metaphorical inferences of its title. . . . You will admit our age (at least our predicament) to be one of transition. If *The Bridge*, embodying as many anomalies as you find in it, yet contains as much authentic poetry here and there as even [Yvor] Winters grants,—then perhaps it can serve as at least the function of a link connecting certain chains of the past to certain chains and tendencies of the future." Crane began with a title and a metaphor, and that is where he ended, together with a poem laboriously and intermittently constituted by that metaphor. But the constitution was imperfect and therefore the poem is uneven and fragmentary. Somewhere between the beginning and end it gets lost. Crane was quite right that a bridge is begun from both ends at once. It also has to meet in the middle, and that is precisely where *The Bridge* buckles.

Slightly past the mid-point of the poem, Crane desperately tries to effectuate a middle by alleging that his reading of Whitman somehow establishes him as Whitman's poetic heir. But in this section of the poem the bridge metaphor is conspicuously forced, and fails to convince either in flat statement:

> To course that span of consciousness thou'st named
> The Open Road—thy vision is reclaimed!

or in apostrophe:

> Our Meistersinger, thou set breath in steel;
> And it was thou who on the boldest heel
> Stood up and flung the span on even wing
> Of that great Bridge, our Myth, whereof I sing!

Ultimately Crane failed to perfect *The Bridge* because he was trying to write out of the wrong tradition. His metaphorical precursor is not Whitman but Emily Dickinson (America's greatest metaphorical mixmaster) and, behind her, Emerson. Throughout his career he was trammeled in the nominalistic, English-imitating tradition of metaphor. Yes, the poem successfully contains visible organic forms: it moves from dawn to midnight, and at the same time from present to past to present again. But these secondary forms are not sufficiently conjoined in the synoptic arc of the bridge, and therefore the entire performance, however beautiful in parts, is structurally unsound. It is a lovely thing to contemplate, but I wouldn't want to risk my life driving a car over it. Neither, I suspect, would Whitman have risked the fate of American poetry crossing a ferry underneath.

William Carlos Williams and
Open-Ended Metaphor

> I have told you, this
> is a fiction, pay attention
>
> WILLIAMS, *Paterson*

THE term constituting metaphor is vulnerable to gross miscalculation if the reader thinks of constitutions only as rigid, static, closed, formal actions, forgetting that good constitutions are equally susceptible of judicial interpretation and later amendment. (Endlessly, in states like California.) Actually, as I have tried to show, even poems of constituting metaphor that appear to be most closed ("When Lilacs Last in the Dooryard Bloom'd," *The Waste Land*) are in our real poetical experience nearly as open as poems that aren't yet finished (the *Cantos*). And it might even be argued, against the tendency of my argument in the preceding section, that *The Bridge* fails less from looseness than from Crane's over-insistence on closing out his metaphor too mechanically. At the opposite extreme, William Carlos Williams' *Paterson* is the best instance in American poetry of a major poem built on constituting metaphor that is at the same time constitutionally open-ended.

Not only as a poem but in its genesis *Paterson* is a happier example of constituting metaphor than *The Bridge*. (Williams had a happier aesthetic.) The genesis of its constituting metaphor is very clearly traced in Williams' *Autobiography* (and again, somewhat differently, in *I Wanted to Write a Poem*). "That is why I started to write *Paterson*: a man is indeed a city, and for the poet there are no ideas but in things. . . . The poet thinks with his poem, in that lies his thought, and that in itself is the profundity. The thought is *Paterson*, to be discovered there. . . . The first idea centering

98

upon the poem, *Paterson*, came alive early: to find an image large enough to embody the whole knowable world about me. . . . I already had the river." ("I took the river as it followed its course down to the sea; all I had to do was follow it and I had a poem," he said in *I Wanted to Write a Poem*. "The poem begins with general observations of the conditions of life in the area. . . . A stream has to begin somewhere. . . . The concept of the beginning of a river is of course a symbol of all beginnings.") All Williams needed now was a particular city. When he chose Paterson he had *Paterson*. "I took the city as my 'case' to work up. . . . It called for a poetry such as I did not know, it was my duty to discover or make such a context on the 'thought.' To *make* a poem, fulfilling the requirements of the art, and yet new, in the sense that in the very lay of the syllables Paterson as Paterson would be discovered, perfect, perfect in the special sense of the poem."

There is the constituting metaphor. In the same passage Williams goes on to touch on my other two subjects, poetic language in America and the meter-making argument. (So impossible is it to divide these three matters, except as chapters in a book.) Of language:

> It would be as itself, locally, and so like every other place in the world. For it is in that, that it be particular to its own idiom, that it lives.
>
> The Falls let out a roar as it crashed upon the rocks. . . . In the imagination this roar is a speech or a voice, a speech in particular; it is the poem itself that is the answer.

And of metric, incidentally returning upon Whitman:

> In the end the man rises from the sea where the river appears to have lost its identity and accompanied by his faithful bitch, obviously a Chesapeake Bay retriever, turns inland toward Cam-

den where Walt Whitman, much traduced, lived the latter years of his life and died. He always said that his poems, which had broken the dominance of the iambic pentameter in English prosody, had only begun his theme. I agree. It is up to us, in the new dialect, to continue it by a new construction upon the syllables.

We always return upon Whitman, who is yet our most perpetually-modern older poet; Williams' last sentence can just as well lead us to Charles Olson's famous essay on "Projective Verse" (1950), with its famous definitions about "composition by field," and thus to much of the best American poetry of the past two decades.

In *Paterson* the diversity of material is more striking than in *The Waste Land* or *The Bridge*, and perhaps even more so than in the *Cantos*. And yet the poem aspires to a very firm unity. As we have seen, *Paterson* is ambitiously—some may think too ambitiously, but I am not among them—held together by a single constituting metaphor, man as city, which Williams finds it necessary to explain and justify in a prefatory note that reads like a constitution:

AUTHOR'S NOTE

Paterson is a long poem in four parts—that a man in himself is a city, beginning, seeking, achieving and concluding his life in ways which the various aspects of a city may embody—if imaginatively conceived—any city, all the details of which may be made to voice his most intimate convictions. Part One introduces the elemental character of the place. The Second Part comprises the modern replicas. Three will seek a language to make them vocal, and Four, the river below the Falls, will be reminiscent of episodes—all that any one man may achieve in a lifetime.

(Let the question of the four or more books lie on the table for the moment. This is Williams' original argument for Books One-Four, and he never retracted it.) To reinforce his constituting metaphor, Williams quotes as a headnote to Book Three a passage from Santayana, *The Last Puritan*, which also argues that "cities are a second body for the human mind, a second organism, more rational, permanent and decorative than the animal organism of flesh and bone: a work of natural yet moral art, where the soul sets up her trophies of action and instruments of pleasure." Williams' point is obviously that his metaphor is not, in a bad sense, "invented" (concocted), but that it is truly "found," truly there in the world. The Santayana passage also enables Williams to assert that both halves of his metaphorical equation are poetic; not merely *Paterson* is poetic but the universal city for which it is metaphorical is itself already poetic.

This is a curious argument but no more so than the Author's Note, of which the syntax of the first "sentence" primarily commands attention. "*Paterson* is a long poem in four parts—that a man in himself is a city," etc. That is not a sentence in the English language but an American constituting metaphor. Williams has deliberately constructed his syntax in such a way that it cannot be reduced to prose logic. Entirely lacking the conjunctions that make English prose possible, the remark has to be read as a metaphor, it has to be simply accepted or rejected as the equivalent of the poem. It *is* the poem. *Paterson* is an independent clause that appears to be part of a sentence but is not. It is precisely a metaphor. It is our old friend the constituting metaphor. Establish that *Paterson* is a poem is a man is a city—thus I violate Williams' metaphor —and it follows in course that "the various aspects of a city," its places, people, activities, etc., may embody all these propositions without further argument, stipulated only—the usual stipulation and danger point of the poem of constituting metaphor—that all these aspects are by the poem, and will be by the well-disposed reader, "imaginatively conceived." To explicate these endless aspects would be futile and superfluous. The poem is more fun to read than any other poem in American poetry, and I have no desire to forestall the reader's pleasure in making his own discoveries, most of which are too obvious for comment anyway:

> Say it! No ideas but in things. Mr.
> Paterson has gone away
> to rest and write. Inside the bus one sees
> his thoughts sitting and standing. His
> thoughts alight and scatter—

If you want me again look for me under your boot-soles. Williams looked and found.

The four promised Books of *Paterson* were published in 1946, 1948, 1949, and 1951. And at first, and for a while, fourness was an essential part of the poem's structure. "Many years ago I was impressed with the four-sided parallelogram," Williams wrote 18 January 1955 to Henry Wells, "in short, with the cube. Shifting at once, to save time, the trinity always seemed unstable. It lacked a fourth member, the devil." Williams was surely thinking of Whitman's "Chanting the Square Deific," which makes the same point. "I found myself always conceiving my abstract designs as possessing four sides. That was natural enough with spring, summer, autumn and winter always before me. To leave any one of them out would have been unthinkable." Here we have an obvious war between space and time designs. Time finally won. Book Five appeared in 1958 and on his death Williams left fragments toward a projected Book Six. As he wrote his publisher: "[since completing *Paterson, Four*] I have come to understand not only that many changes have occurred in me and the world, but I have been forced to recognize that there can be no end to such a story I have envisioned with the terms which I had laid down for myself. I had to take the world of Paterson into a new dimension if I wanted to give it imaginative validity. Yet I wanted to keep it whole, as it is to me." Williams deliberately blew his parallelogram, upon which he had so insisted in his letter to Wells. Yet in the same letter he virtually predicted what was bound to happen. "I conceived the whole of *Paterson* at one stroke and wrote it down—as it appears at the beginning of the poem. All I had to do after that was to fill in the details as I went along, from day to day." By blowing the parallelogram, yet each to keep and all, William blew his constituting metaphor wide open at the forward-looking end, thereby achieving what was impossible even for pioneer Whitman (traditional effects require more predecessors than Whitman had)—not a cube but something immeasurably more entertaining and valuable, an epitome of American poetry from the point of view of constituting metaphor, down to his own time and open to the future.

Chapter Three

WHAT THE THUNDER SAID

Voices and the Primitive Terror

What are the roots that clutch, what branches grow
Out of this stony rubbish? Son of man,
You cannot say, or guess, for you know only
A heap of broken images.

T. S. Eliot, *The Waste Land*

"I HAVE TOLD you, this/ is a fiction, pay attention," as aforesaid by Williams. Let the vegetation stand for American poetry, root and branch, and let the stony rubbish stand for the American poet's rock-bottom sense of his dislocation from the English heritage (language, sensibility, literature, culture, politics). Let the heap of broken images stand for our anfractuous American poems. The epigraph is Eliot's first indentation (paragraph break) in "I. The Burial of the Dead," summary comment on the opening eighteen lines of broken images, a conspicuous medley of dictions (including German—*echt deutsch, echt amerikan*), which run the gamut from the fatuously masochistic parody of Chaucer ("April is the cruellest month") to the masochistically fatuous colloquialism of "I read, much of the night, and go south in the winter." The passage is haunted by memories of Poe and Whitman "breeding/ Lilacs out of the dead land"; haunted much more by the ghostly melange of styles, traditional and conversational, each imperiously declaring its want of authority. The branches that grow from this stony rubbish grow from the pluralistic juxtapositions (American Eclectic) that reach a kind of definitive hysteria in the concluding lines of the poem. It seems to me a grand mistake to assume that the last-minute triune benedictions of Shantih conclude anything. There is no peace which passeth understanding in *The Waste Land* unless it is in the meditations of the gramophone-playing typist. London Bridge, and the English language, are falling down, and Hieronymo's mad again; north-north-west; knows a hack from a handsaw.

Eliot turned away, not so much from America to England as from poetry to drama, but still compels our imagination:

> And the ragged rock in the restless waters,
> Waves wash over it, fogs conceal it;
> On a halcyon day it is merely a monument,
> In navigable weather it is always a seamark
> To lay a course by: but in the sombre season
> Or the sudden fury, is what it always was.

However it may be with the meters and metaphors, American poetry has in the depths of its language few halcyon days, but mainly the sombre season and the sudden fury, "the backward half-look/ Over the shoulder, towards the primitive terror," as Eliot says a few lines earlier. Simple history. A new and relatively unpopulated continent, an alien and imported language brought by an invasion force unable or unwilling to assimilate Indian culture or language, and daily losing linguistic touch with the mother country, increasingly compelled to face the unknown with a language inorganically related to it. The Americans have always confronted the primitive terror with an uneasy language, either speechless or talking out of both sides of their mouths. Eventually, of course, they had to invent a new language, but within strict limits, for, as we have seen, it is a pretty poor play on words to speak of an American language unrelated to English.[1]

---

[1] The problem is not restricted to the Western Hemisphere but extends as far as the European (or other) colonial powers imposed their linguistic culture on other people. Thus Stephen Daedalus reflects in James Joyce, *A Portrait of the Artist as a Young Man* (1914): "The language in which we are speaking is his before it is mine. How different are the words *home, Christ, ale, master,* on his lips and on mine! . . . His language, so familiar

And the situation is much worse with language than with meters or metaphors. Lacking his rhythm or his form, a man is gauche and uncontrolled; lacking a language, he is nearly out of his mind. The final agony of the American poets is of course poetic diction.[2]

In a poem aptly if only half-consciously called "Esthétique du Mal," Wallace Stevens, as usual, lets the American hellcat out of the bag:

> Natives of poverty, children of malheur,
> The gaiety of language is our seigneur.

(With *droits*.) Typically, Stevens cannot even speak his own vocabulary, but must, like weak Whitman, go whoring after the Roman vernaculars, only to meet his overmatch. There are "two grand practical distinctions" in the writing of history, Melville remarks in *Pierre*, introducing a chapter on "Young America in Literature." The two modes can stand for just about anything—England and America, for example, since the distinction turns on chronological order vs timeless contemporaneity—and of them Melville loftily observes: "I elect neither of these; I am careless of either; both are well enough in their way; I write precisely as I please." Well, hardly. The American witness is too God-intoxicated and word-martyred to be quenched by Melvillean heroism (or by Melville's reactionary Emerson-style poetry either). Through all the "tide of voices—/ ... The long, tired sounds, fog-insulated noises:/ Gongs in white

---

and so foreign, will always be for me an acquired speech. I have not made or accepted its words. My voice holds them at bay. My soul frets in the shadow of his language."

[2] The reader should be advised at outset that I use the term "poetic diction" broadly, ranging from such relatively inconsequential matters as word choice to such ultimate issues as the question whether a human being can maintain his integrity unless he can modulate and hear the true sound of his own voice and his neighbors'.

surplices, beshrouded wails," it breaks forth almost incoherently in Hart Crane's *The Bridge*, in the very song following the over-strained invocation to "Walt" ("Ascensions of thee hover in me now"):

> It is blood to remember; it is fire
> To stammer back . . . It is
> God—your namelessness. And the wash—

Expatriate Eliot, when not befogged by Dr. Johnson's London ("The word neither diffident nor ostentatious,/ An easy commerce of the old and the new,/ The common word exact without vulgarity,/ The formal word precise but not pedantic,/ The complete consort dancing together"), speaks more clearly, perhaps because at a distance he feels less immediately threatened:

> Words strain,
> Crack and sometimes break, under the burden,
> Under the tension, slip, slide, perish,
> Decay with imprecision, will not stay in place,
> Will not stay still.

As in Poe, "still" means "silent" in addition to "stay in place." There immediately follow "shrieking voices/ Scolding, mocking, or merely chattering,/ . . . The Word in the desert/ . . . voices of temptation,/ The crying shadow in the funeral dance,/ The loud lament of the disconsolate chimera." In the opening section of the same poem ("Burnt Norton") a bird (after echoes) seduces us ("shall we follow/ The deception of the thrush? Into our first world") into a garden (virgin land, despite British landscaping), only to turn on us at the end, like a minuscule Moby Dick:

> Go, go, go, said the bird: human kind
> Cannot bear very much reality.

The Americans have no choice. In Williams' poem *Paterson*, Mrs. Cumming, faced with the roaring abyss of the Passaic Falls, shrieked and plunged to her death, either because she had a false language or none. At least she was in good company. A lot of minor poets had gone before.

The Early American Poets and Poetic Diction

Personally, I like words to sound wrong.

WALLACE STEVENS, letter of 1 June 1939

BECAUSE they seldom unify their poems through constituting metaphor, British poets of the nineteenth and twentieth centuries tend to find their unity, which is superficially much more striking than the unity of American poems, in a unity of tone that derives from poetic diction and is further corroborated by the regularity of British metric. British poems by the same poet tend to sound more alike than American poems by the same poet. They also tend to sound more or less the same all the way through, whereas an American poem often sounds at first hearing as if it had been patched together by a committee. Even the verbal eccentricities of British mavericks—Browning, Hopkins, Dylan Thomas—appear constrained and docile in comparison with the linguistic atrocities perpetrated by their barbarous overseas contemporaries. The representative British poem flows as evenly as the Isis. The representative American poem is notorious for rapids, cataracts, whirlpools, portages, and quicksands.

It has not always been so. After all, the American literary revolution lagged behind the American political revolution by about two generations. It also lagged, by a shorter stretch of time, slightly less than two generations,[3] behind the British revolution in poetic diction

[3] Generations are of course impossible to define, but here is a brief list of suggestive dates:

1776 Declaration of Independence	1817 Bryant, "Thanatopsis"
1787 Constitutional Convention	1827 Poe, *Tamerlane and*
1798 Wordsworth and Coleridge,	*Other Poems*
Lyrical Ballads	1836 Emerson, *Nature*
1807 Barlow, *The Columbiad*	

112

engineered by Wordsworth and Coleridge. That revolution established a perdurable stylistic tradition of harmony and subjugation and flow decidedly at odds with the choppy but flashing local brilliance of Dryden and Pope, a tradition in which neither single words nor combinations of words were permitted to assert their singularity against the imperial unity of tone of the whole poem. (Meanwhile the American poets down to Bryant went on writing like Dryden and Pope.) Nineteenth- and twentieth-century British poetry is in broadest outlines a poetry still in the Wordsworth-Coleridge mode, held in close and continuing relationship with British prose and in decorous and continuing relationship with British speech.

By the time of Bryant, American poetry had caught up with the tamer and duller sides of the British Romantic revolution, and for a few years the new British way sounded ideally adapted to native ears. On the whole, American outrages in diction go hand in hand with American outrages in meter, and where there is no sign of the one there is little use searching for the other. Predictably Bryant stands four-square and flat-footed on the new British tradition. However various their ostensible topics (there isn't much variety) or their external forms (stanzas and that kind of thing), all Bryant's poems sound remarkably alike, partly because they all sound like Wordsworth, whose poems also sound remarkably alike. Moreover, within the individual poems there is scarcely a ruffle in diction. It is as if the Bryant poem emerged from a computer programmed with a Basic English for poetry, a vocabulary selected with the prime purpose of preventing any single word from ever colliding with any conceivable combination of other words. "Thanatopsis" so beautifully maintains its impassive and tranquil tone of voice (if voice it is) that it usually goes without notice how awkwardly and inorganically the poem lurches between third-person declarative and second-person imperative modes. And what Bryant preached was even worse than what he practiced. Inconsistently objecting to American poets who borrow their styles from single British poets, Bryant goes on to a terrible concession (in a book review of 1818): "Still less

113

would we be understood as intending to censure that sort of imitation which, exploring all the treasures of English poetry, culls from all a diction, that shall form a natural and becoming dress for the conceptions of the writer,—this is a course of preparation which every one ought to go through." Naturally, every poet ought to read. But why should he "cull"? Worst of all, it sounds suspiciously as if Bryant were culling rather more with his eye than his ear. There is little enough evidence in his poems that he ever heard anything that was going on around him in the United States (in business since 1776).

Meanwhile, in real life, owing to geographical isolation, the impact of other ethnic groups, anti-British sentiment (whipped up again by the War of 1812), and doubtless many other factors, the United States was slowly becoming less English. Gradually, American speech began its long course of slow development away from British norms. Increasingly the Americans' ears got out of tune with English verse, which was going its own way, in its own forwards-backwards traditional fashion, and certainly not in the direction of America. Therefore in diction, as in meter, the brief moment of Bryant conformity was necessarily followed by an Age of Growing Discomfort and Inadequate Remedy (Poe, Emerson, Lowell), which persisted until the ailment was finally diagnosed and lanced by Whitman. The early national assumption of a single English poetry, unified by a common language, divided into two separate and unequal branches by geography and political independence, collapsed. There followed an uneasy interim in which the more ambitious talents writhed in the bondage of British diction, and sought, for the most part unsuccessfully, to escape its overwhelming authority. As always, the American political situation created the problem and supplied the answer, but no one before Whitman fully understood that the political challenge could only be met by a poetical answer.

Lacking that revolutionary understanding, the interim poets

114

naturally experienced a kind of unspeakable frustration, which could never be openly voiced because it could be neither accepted nor escaped, and which therefore shows in the poetry mainly as a symptom of dislocation. Much of Poe's awkwardness is a deliberate attempt to destroy, since he can neither live with nor resolve nor (except on rare occasion) transcend the dilemma posed for the native poet by an imported poetic diction. As in the case of metric, it is sheer idiocy to ascribe Poe's awkwardness to mere poetical ineptitude. No, the awkwardness is an act of will, an aggressive movement made against an intolerable situation, and it is notably sporadic. Poe can write as smoothly (an easy thing, despite our text-books) as Shelley or Keats when he feels like it. Like Melville's Bartleby, he prefers not to. His ear, the American ear in general, was virtually itching to be outraged; consequently Poe's small poetic oeuvre is a little treasure-chest of linguistic outrages. As if to empha-size the degree of his enormities, Poe regularly underscores his most anarchic diction with heavy alliteration or, most mortal of poetical sins, with rhyme. No man arrived at the years of discretion ever out of simple ineptitude wrote such a line as the following (from "The City in the Sea"):

The viol, the violet, and the vine.

The line is a highly self-conscious attempt to parody and attack a presumably agreed-upon tradition of poetic language in which such things are simply "not done." No other explanation can ever make sense of such a rhyme scheme (in "Israfel") as "levin-even-seven-Heaven." Only one of the four words ("Heaven") in any way suits the context, and, moreover, the one bad rhyme ("even") is of all the four words the most aggressively and superfluously lugged in. There is perhaps no aspect of poetry less commonly understood than this matter of rhyming. With a poet as good as Poe—with poets incom-

115

parably less good than Poe—"bad" rhyming is not a technical lapse but an aesthetic statement and action. Poe was not required to rhyme "October" and "Auber" in "Ulalume," nor "volcanic" and "Yaanek." Indeed, he must have thought long and hard, searched far and wide, for so repellent a set of combinations.

Poe's aggressiveness did not of course always result in repulsion. In "Ulalume," the rhyme progression "senescent-liquescent-crescent" is decidedly organic to the purposes of the poem, and unusually successful. Finally in "The Raven" Poe beat the British on their own grounds. (The most obvious source of the poem is Elizabeth Barrett's "Lady Geraldine's Courtship.") He simply carried to excess internal and end rhyming, thus freeing the words from their literal meaning, and breaking through to a new kind of music. Every American knows the sound of "The Raven" from childhood, and carries that sound with him until the day he dies, despite the nearly universal disapproval of critics and teachers. Consequently most American readers of poetry find themselves frustrated and confused by a situation in which they secretly like a poem they ought not to admire. Perhaps the easiest way around this quandary is first to listen a while to the excessive internal and end rhyming of T. S. Eliot, who probably got it from Poe, and which no critic that I know of has ever objected to, or probably even heard. (Eliot's double enveloped rhyme in "Ash Wednesday," "The token of the word unheard, unspoken," may well have its genesis in an unconscious childhood or adolescent memory of a line in "The Raven," "But the silence was unbroken, and the stillness gave no token.") A more direct way out of the quandary is to listen to Poe:

> Once upon a midnight dreary, while I pondered,
> weak and weary,
> Over many a quaint and curious volume of forgotten lore—
> While I nodded, nearly napping, suddenly
> there came a tapping,

116

> As of some one gently rapping, rapping at my chamber door—
> " 'Tis some visitor," I muttered, "tapping at my
>   chamber door—
>   Only this and nothing more."

I have no heart for an elaborate critical proof. The reader who can't hear that can't hear anything. Of course, he has to read it right. Read as tub-thump, it comes out tub-thump. Read with close attention to the intricate prose patterning that Poe plays against his meter, it comes out Beauty, which is all Poe was ever after. What he got this time was a new music that also satisfies the Ford Madox Ford-Ezra Pound requirement that poetry be as well written as prose. The stanza just quoted is the first, since I didn't want to prejudice the case by searching out the "best" one. Most of the others end with the word "Nevermore." In "The Philosophy of Composition," Poe's account of the genesis of "The Raven" boils down to this single word. Poe says he determined "length, the province and the tone," and then betook himself to ordinary induction. Ordinary induction led him to the refrain, to the desirable brevity of the refrain, to the desirability of its being a single word ("sonorous and susceptible of protracted emphasis"), and thus to "Nevermore." He had then to imagine a "pretext for the continuous use of the one word," and his poem was accomplished. Curiously, but not at all accidentally, the single word[4] gave him his constituting metaphor (the Raven as "emblematical of *Mournful and Never-ending Remembrance*"). It was an extraordinary choice. As William Carlos Williams, the only one of our modern poets to take Poe seriously (in public), cunningly remarks: "[Poe's] passion for the refrain is like an echo from a hollow. It is his own voice returning" (*In the American Grain*).

Less daring in practice than Poe, though not less awkward, Emer-

---

[4] How seriously and, in his predicament, pedantically, Poe took the single word is everywhere evident in his criticism, where he is always picking away at diction (when he is not picking away at meter).

117

son must still claim the honor of having first adumbrated an American theory of poetic diction. (Poe had no real theory, just an instinct and an ear. Lacking the instinct and the ear, Emerson wrote no "Raven." He was a thinker.) The theory is in the chapter on "Language" in *Nature* (1836); it has been much quoted in other connections, usually metaphysical; it is blessedly brief:

1. Words are signs of natural facts.
2. Particular natural facts are symbols of particular spiritual facts.
3. Nature is the symbol of spirit.

The philosophical and philological merit of these propositions may be waived, but not their poetical or historical interest. Taken in relation to each other as organic parts of a single statement, what the three propositions amount to is that language is the natural (realistic) symbol (metaphor) of spirit (meaning). Or to let Emerson speak further: "The world is emblematic. Parts of speech are metaphors, because the whole of nature is a metaphor of the human mind. The laws of moral nature answer to those of matter as face to face in a glass. . . . This relation between the mind and matter is not fancied by some poet, but stands in the will of God, and so is free to be known by all men. It appears to men, or it does not appear." This was lifelong doctrine. Years later Emerson wrote: "The value of a trope is that the hearer is one: and indeed Nature itself is a vast trope, and all particular natures are tropes. . . . All thinking is analogizing, and it is the use of life to learn metonymy. The endless passing of one element into new forms, the incessant metamorphosis, explains the rank which the imagination holds in our catalogue of mental powers. The imagination is the reader of these forms" ("Poetry and Imagination").

The doctrine is at once cosmic and nominalistic, and it makes quite clear why Emerson did not follow, or precede, Whitman in the discovery of the constituting metaphor. For Emerson, the universe was already constituted—elsewhere he said otherwise, of course—and its poetry inhered in the metaphor found in the single word or phrase; the same frame of mind turns up in such Emersonian people as Melville, Dickinson, and Hart Crane. Emerson's doctrine was corroborated by the way he read poetry. Theoretically the imagination might be the reader of forms, but the forms Emerson read were fragments. He read poems for their lines or images, not for their poetic wholes. His essays are full of revelatory remarks on his reading habits: "The adventitious beauty of poetry may be felt in the greater delight which a verse gives in happy quotation than in the poem" ("Art," *Society and Solitude*); "The reason we set so high a value on any poetry,—as often on a line or a phrase as on a poem,—is that it is a new work of Nature, as a man is" ("Poetry and Imagination"); "Poetry. . . . All its words are poems" ("Poetry and Imagination"); "I wish that the poet should foresee this habit of readers, and omit all but the important passages" ("Poetry and Imagination"); "In reading prose, I am sensitive as soon as a sentence drags; but in poetry, as soon as one word drags" ("Poetry and Imagination").

Therefore Emerson wrote in "The Poet," luring Whitman and many another lapsed Adamic poet after him, "bare lists of words are found suggestive to an imaginative and excited mind." Leaving aside Emerson's deliriously magical view of the poet as "namer," let us inquire into the practical bearing of his theory on American poetic diction. The answer is simple and obvious, though it comes in two parts. (1) American diction will be realistic, common, prosaic, bare, and, contrariwise—given the mysteries of nature—exotic, bizarre, polyglot, and *outré* (as it already was in Poe). It will show little or no sense of decorum. Decorum is God's business. (2) Unless countervailed by some such principle as the constituting metaphor, American poetic diction will be almost exhibitionistically particular. It will dote upon and flaunt the single word. It will use the single word in lieu of a developed metaphor. It will " 'mount to paradise/ By the stairway of surprise' " ("Merlin"), sometimes skipping the stairs.

Lowell was as usual brilliantly wrong in alleging that Emerson's verse was "not even prose." Prose is precisely what it is, a witty, epigrammatic prose continuous with the "grand verse" (Lowell still) of the great early essays. On the other hand, Lowell observed accurately when he said that "in the worst of his poems are mines of rich matter,/ But thrown in a heap with a crash and a clatter;/ Now it is not one thing nor another alone/ Makes a poem, but rather the general tone." (Good example of Lowell at the mercy of the British tradition.) However it may sort with Emerson's oversoul-overview of the universe, Emerson's verse has very little poetic, but only discursive, unity. He is the majority leader of the flashing fragment. When he does occasionally rise above argumentative prose it is in the single line, phrase, or word, and consequently we find one kind of American poetry (usually in the conservative tradition) indwelling in such fast passes as these: "The journeying atoms"; "She melted into purple cloud,/ She silvered in the moon;/ She spired into a yellow flame;/ She flowered in blossoms red;/ She flowed into a foaming wave:/ She stood Monadnoc's head"; "the whited air"; "tumultuous privacy of storm"; "The frolic architecture of the snow"; "As the two twilights of the day/ Fold us music-drunken in"; "Expound the Vedas of the violet." We are already halfway to "the agile precincts of the lark's return." Single, isolated words simply scream for attention, and in most cases the screaming word is its own metaphorical excuse for being, comparatively unrelated to anything else. This is the poetry of the instantaneous, timeless illumination. It is the exact reverse of the British tradition of harmony and subjugation and flow. Especially in more accomplished poets than Emerson it may be a poetry of piercing and haunting and transient loveliness, but it cannot build a coherent poetical world.

Lowell, who tried his hand at everything else, also tried his hand

120

at the problem of American diction, and was, as usual, bested. The dialect poems of *The Biglow Papers*—any dialect poems, for that matter—represent the *reductio ad absurdum* of the Americans' linguistic dilemma. Still, the long Introduction he wrote for the Second Series in 1867 is an essential key to the Age of Growing Discomfort and Inadequate Remedy and must not be overlooked. The problem is of course British imitation. "It had long seemed to me that the great vice of American writing and speaking was a studied want of simplicity," wrote Lowell, sounding almost like a proto-Whitman, until we remember that Lowell and Whitman spoke to different kinds of people, "that we were in danger of coming to look on our mother-tongue as a dead language . . . and that our only chance of escape was by seeking it at its living sources among those who were . . . 'divinely illiterate.' " That is a better description than a diagnosis. Lowell does not seriously inquire what *is* our mother tongue nor why there was a danger of finding mother dead some day. Neither does he mean what Whitman might have meant by "divinely illiterate." When Whitman praised "illiteracy," he was referring to the poetic power of Dante, not to some country farmer allegedly still speaking the language of the Coventry Plays. It is doubtless the unholy alliance between Harvard philology and gimmick poetics that is wrenching Lowell's critical judgment awry, for elsewhere he comes close to defining the national dilemma: "We use it [our native language; but he does not mean the American variety of the English language; he means *English*] like Scotsmen, not as if it belonged to us, but as if we wished to prove that we belong to it. . . . And yet all the while our popular idiom is racy with life and vigor and originality." That was of course true, as Whitman had long since demonstrated, though probably it was more true on Brooklyn ferries than in the Harvard Yard, but Lowell disapproved of Whitman and learned nothing from him; what Lowell lacked was the talent of application. "No language after it has faded into *diction* . . . can bring forth a sound and lusty book." But however American he was in certain selected sentiments, Lowell simply could not separate himself, or recognize his de facto separation from the English sensibility enshrined in English literature. "There is death in the dictionary," he added, failing to see the equal death in an anachronistic dialect poetry justified as more ancient than the English. What had happened to the divine average, the way real people really spoke in the United States, as opposed to rural New England? Pandering to a sectional illiteracy, Lowell was in fact pandering to a regressive and politically reactionary view of the English language, totally overlooking the political and poetical realities of the post-Revolutionary nation, even while in the noble act of excoriating that nation for the "national crime" of the Mexican War.

The Birth of Death in Whitman

The high ones die, die. They die. You look up and who's there?
—Easy, easy, Mr Bones. I is on your side.
I smell your grief.
—I sent my grief away. I cannot care
forever. With them all again & again I died
and cried, and I have to live.

JOHN BERRYMAN, 36 of *The Dream Songs*

THAT THERE is something intrinsically dialectic about the problem of diction in American poetry becomes immediately evident in the discrepancy between Whitman's prose statements and poetical practice, on the one hand, and his poetical themes on the other. Neither in the prose statements—except in a rare moment: "the great radical Republic . . . its loud, ill-pitch'd voice" ("Poetry To-Day—Shakspere—The Future")—nor in the language of the poems does there seem to be any problem at all, whereas the thematic drift of the poems is exquisitely problematical. Even in *An American Primer*, written, but unfinished, during the years of the early editions of *Leaves of Grass* (c. 1850-60), in which Whitman is doggedly trying to Americanize the English language, there is no sign of strain. From "Song of Myself" forward, Whitman simply draws upon whatever vocabularies he likes, mainly the American vernacular, but also archaicisms, poeticisms, neologisms, foreign borrowings, new coinages, slang, and toward this psychedelic eclecticism of vocabularies he maintains an attitude of imperturbable tranquillity. "There is that indescribable freshness and unconsciousness about an illiterate person that humbles and mocks the power of the noblest expressive genius" (1855 preface). Needless to say, Whitman is the expressive genius and the "illiterate person" the ever-

123

ready, ever-malleable language of his fellow human being. For all his psychedelic eclecticism. Whitman is usually best at his simplest, which is when he is closest to the vernacular and at the same time being more artful than Poe:

> When the psalm sings instead of the singer,
> When the script preaches instead of the preacher,
> When the pulpit descends and goes instead of the carver
>   that carved the supporting desk,
> When the sacred vessels or the bits of the eucharist,
>   or the lath and plast, procreate as effectually
>   as the young silversmiths or bakers,
>   or the masons in their overalls,
> When a university course convinces like a slumbering woman
>   and child convince,
> When the minted gold in the vault smiles
>   like the nightwatchman's daughter,
> When warrantee deeds loafe in chairs opposite
>   and are my friendly companions,
> I intend to reach them my hand and make as much of them
>   as I do of men and women.

The last line is a good average example of Whitman's art. Every word is simple and ordinary and all the words are in the simplest, easiest order. The line falls into three more or less equal phrasings. "I intend to reach them my hand," "and make as much of them," "as I do of men and women." The phrasings can either be taken as separate lines or as one long line. Taken as one long line it is a nine-foot iambic line, with three anapestic substitutions and a feminine ending. Taken as phrasings, they add up to three fairly regular iambic trimeters. And yet it is all simplicity itself. (Compare Dante's "economy of words" and "the tangled and florid Shakespeare.")

There are to be in Whitman's poems no "abstract addresses," a point readily checked out by comparison of actual Whitman poems with such Whitman-like poems (they contain moaning of one kind or another) as "Tintern Abbey," "Ulysses," or "Dover Beach," all properly garbed as they are in the standard British poetical style of address, abstract, haughty, rhetorical, hypermetric, randomly metaphorical. "The gaggery and gilt of a million years will not prevail. Who troubles himself about his ornaments or fluency is lost." This is the Whitman—and thus the radical American—party line, perfectly controlled, self-poised and venomous toward the threatening British tradition. Even when it is a question of the human voice, or of the nature of sound—the true key to American poetic diction—a superficial, truculent confidence reigns: "from the voice [the human voice] proceeds another voice [the poetic voice] eternally curious of the harmony of things with man." What could be more democratically self-assured? "To speak in literature with the perfect rectitude and insouciance of the movements of animals . . . is the flawless triumph of art." Perhaps we have not yet looked with the proper rectitude and insouciance at this flawless prose. The poet, Whitman goes on, "swears to his art. . . . I will not have in my writing any elegance or effect or originality [back of the hand to Poe] to hang in the way between me and the rest like curtains. . . . What I tell I tell for precisely what it is." Even when conceding a point, Whitman hews to this absolutely organic and democratic aesthetic: "those ornaments can be allowed that conform to the perfect facts of the open air and that flow out of the nature of the work." Yankee clippers, skyscrapers, American one-upmanship. Unlike the situation in meter and metaphor, the inherited, shared, quarreled-over English language is accommodation itself. "The English language befriends the grand American expression. . . . It is the medium that shall well nigh express the inexpressible." Or so it seems; on second thought, people sometimes "befriend" people toward whom they feel sorry or condescending.[5] Still and all—for what American critic would willingly impale himself upon so delicate a barb?—Whitman's tone is as calm and placid as a Poe lake, complete with lolling water lilies. "With the twirl of my tongue I encompass worlds and volumes of worlds." The doctrines of the 1855 preface exactly tally the doctrines and practices of the 1855 poems. "Gab and . . . loitering," "The sound of the belched words of my voice," "I too am untranslatable,/ I sound my barbaric yawp over the roofs of the world." All this is transparent irony. The yawp is untranslatable because it stands in no need of translation. It is simply American poetry, which is the same thing as the sound of the English language in America. "Speech is the twin of my vision." Whitman would soon learn different.

Dates are a necessary nuisance. The breakthrough in meter was in 1855. The breakthrough in metaphor was in 1856 ("Crossing Brooklyn Ferry"). (Or, if the reader prefers, 1845, "The Raven.") The breakthrough in diction was c. 1859, at about which time Whit-

[5] It is perhaps not surprising, but it is certainly discouraging, to find such confusion about their language among even the better American poets. (Doubtless the problem is insoluble; still.) Hart Crane: "the expression of such [modern, American] values may often be as well accomplished with the vocabulary and blank verse of the Elizabethans" ("General Aims and Theories"). William "culling" Bryant, a century earlier: "It has been urged by some, as an obstacle to the growth of elegant literature among us, that our language is a transplanted one, framed for a country and for institutions different from ours, and, therefore, not likely to be wielded by us with such force, effect, and grace, as it would have been if it had grown up with our nation, and received its forms and its accessions from the exigencies of our experience. It seems to me that this is one of the most unsubstantial of all the brood of phantoms which have been conjured up to alarm us. . . . To try this notion about a transplanted dialect, imagine one of the great living poets of England emigrated to this country. Can anybody be simple enough to suppose that his poetry would be the worse for it?" "On Poetry in its Relation to Our Age and Country," *Lectures on Poetry*, 1826. It is hard to imagine anyone more completely missing the point.

man wrote "As I Ebb'd With the Ocean of Life" and "Out of the Cradle Endless Rocking." Nobody seems to know which he wrote first, but "As I Ebb'd With the Ocean of Life" sounds prefatory to me. Since I am talking about something that happened in 1859 I quote the earliest volume publication of the poems in the third edition (1860).[6] In 1855 Whitman assumed that there was no problem of diction in American poetry, that is, that Americans could simply diverge as they liked within the English language, building mainly on the American vernacular, and well-nigh express the inexpressible —themselves; and he had proved it in his poems. By 1859 he knew that the problem of poetic diction had little or nothing to do with vocabulary. He was now face to face with the primitive terror. (Americans had of course been facing the terror since 1607 or earlier, and far more intensely since 1776. But they left no decent records.)

Biographers conjecture that Whitman suffered some traumatic personal experience just before these poems were written. We do not know what experience. We do know from the poems how Whitman got face to face with the primitive terror: he looked hard and honestly within himself and came back with the answer. If the Americans were to escape the second death (Hell) they would have to go through a first death now. And already it was nearly too late. In "As I Ebb'd With the Ocean of Life" Whitman does not really give us the answer, but he prepares us for it. Clearly, this is a poem about personal and cultural identity, the voice and the abyss, primal howls and civilized articulation. It takes the form of a contest between the ocean, "the fierce old mother," the old birth-death double, who "endlessly cries for her castaways," as she will continue to do down into our contemporary poetry, and, countermanding, defiance and failure and belt-tightening and reconsecration on the part of a poet who has conceivably heard too much of "the dirge, the voices of men and

---

[6] Easily available in the facsimile edition edited by Roy Harvey Pearce (Ithaca, New York: Cornell University Press, 1961).

127

women wrecked." But it is not merely a social dirge, it is also the "sobbing dirge of Nature" herself. The "gab" of 1855 has given way to the "blab" of 1860, which in the course of the poem further reduces to "dab."

> O baffled, balked,
> Bent to the very earth, here preceding what follows,
> Oppressed with myself that I have dared to open my mouth,
> Aware now, that, amid all the blab whose echoes
> > recoil upon me, I have not once had the least idea
> > who or what I am,
> But that before all my insolent poems the real ME still
> > stands untouched, untold, altogether unreached,
> Withdrawn far, mocking me with mock-congratulatory
> > signs and bows,
> With peals of distant ironical laughter at every word
> > I have written or shall write,
> Striking me with insults till I fall helpless upon the sand.

The contest has no conclusion except in its poetic quality, which is far more complex and deeply moving than anything Whitman had written before. Because Whitman has exchanged his earlier end-stopped line for a line which is grammatically end-stopped but poetically run-on, it is necessary to quote at some length the end of the poem (anyway, it's one of the great moments in American poetry):

> Me and mine!
> We, loose winrows, little corpses,
> Froth, snowy white, and bubbles,
> (See! from my dead lips the ooze exuding at last!
> See—the prismatic colors, glistening and rolling!)
> Tufts of straw, sands, fragments,
> Buoyed hither from many moods, one contradicting another,

From the storm, the long calm, the darkness, the swell,
Musing, pondering, a breath, a briny tear, a dab
        of liquid or soil,
Up just as much out of fathomless workings
        fermented and thrown,
A limp blossom or two, torn, just as much over waves
        floating, drifted at random,
Just as much for us that sobbing dirge of Nature,
Just as much, whence we come, that blare
        of the cloud-trumpets;
We, capricious, brought hither, we know not whence,
        spread out before You, up there, walking or sitting,
Whoever you are—we too lie in drifts at your feet.

(The capitalized You is, as usual in Whitman, puzzling. It might be God. More likely, it is the reader of the future. The capitalized second-person pronoun is equally stunning, either way.) For American purposes, and as it sounds in my ear, these lines are better than anything in English poetry—excluding Shakespeare, but only in his plays, which are not poems but "poetic" drama, an altogether different genre—and therefore they represent, as well as any single passage can, the exact moment when Whitman, representing the United States, beat English literature to its knees and left it behind, as he had sworn he would, and as was bound to happen sooner or later, given the historical situation.

But the best is yet to come. In this poem Whitman virtually announces another poem. He will throw himself upon the breast of his father Long Island, and hold firm "till you answer me something." The answer is given, but Whitman does not reveal what it is, except indirectly in the concluding lines of the poem just quoted. "O, I will yet sing, some day, what you have said to me," he promises, and he keeps his promise in "A Word Out of the Sea" ("Out of the Cradle Endlessly Rocking"), which is almost certainly, with *Paterson*, the richest document in the philosophy of American poetic diction. It is also the announcement of the triumphant birth of an entire American poetry surpassing the English, whereas the earlier poem celebrated the victory of a single poet only. As in so many American poems about language it is a poem about birthing, especially as birthing can be envisaged simultaneously with dying.[7]

Like many a Poe poem, "A Word Out of the Sea" is narrative, and must be taken in narrative order. It opens with a rocked cradle, the mockingbird's throat, "the musical shuttle," the womb, the nipples of the mother's breasts. Something is being born here, and what it is is poetry. At first it is all very tentative, mere "fitful risings and fallings," "those beginning notes of sickness and love," which yet engender "the thousand responses of my heart," with "the myriad thence-aroused words," including "the word stronger and more delicious than any," which is not disclosed at this point in the poem. It all takes place on "sterile sands," where light and shadow twine and twist "as if they were alive," or as if they were coming from a Poe story. I have been quoting from the epic invocation which introduces the narrative proper. The epic invocation is a long, brilliantly complicated, single sentence in the present tense. When we move to the narrative, which is separately titled "Reminiscence," we move to past tense and to an explanation of how we got this way.

"Once," in May, when the poet was a boy, he found a bird's nest and two birds. All summer he listened and watched, but early on the bird-song changed from a happy duet to a tragic solo. The she-bird disappeared, "may-be killed," nobody knows. As is already evident

---

[7] In the previous chapter I briefly asserted that a crone is not a sentimental image, referring, of course, to the much contested parenthetical penultimate line that Whitman added to later versions: "(Or like some old crone rocking the cradle, swathed in sweet garments, bending aside)". The emendation is an obvious attempt to clarify and enforce the central point of the poem, the birth-death nexus. A crone is a withered old woman, not a nursemaid, and the word is apparently associated with Dutch and French words for "carrion" and "carcass." "Swathed" gives us the Christ-child.

the basic situation is the basic Poe situation, inexplicable death and the loss of love. Everything in the poem has a voice, except the missing she-bird, who offers the opposite of voice, silence. The action takes place "in the sound of the sea," a "hoarse surging." But the boy hears mainly the he-bird, who "poured forth the meanings which *I, of all men,* know." (My emphasis.) As the evidence mounts, I think it will become quite apparent that the he-bird is Poe, and that Whitman is saying that he of all men now understands what Poe suffered, perhaps more than even Poe understood it, and is going to redeem and purify it for posterity, thereby making himself into a greater poet than Poe, yes, but also enshrining Poe as the inarticulate originator of the American poetic tradition. Whitman fictively listens, treasuring every note, "Recalling now the obscure shapes, the echoes, the sounds and sights after their sorts,/ The white arms out in the breakers tirelessly tossing/ . . . now translating the notes,/ Following you, my brother."

The brothers are closely related but not identical. To the boy the waves "slap," but to the bird they "*lap.*" (Whitman used italics on "*lap,*" and all the other italicized words quoted below, to discriminate the bird's song from the rest of the poem. There is no question of emphasis.) The word that the bird apparently hears in the surf is "*soothe,*" which is not the word the boy is going to hear. The bird's futile simplistic voice is loud, high, and clear, but it overshoots the waves. Or he modulates his voice to a "*murmur,*" asking the "*husky-noised sea*" to be quiet a moment and still nothing happens, not even when he modulates his voice to a "*just-sustained note.*" Naturally, there is no response. Except for Whitman nobody is listening. The audience is either dead or gone away. Moreover there is an unconquerable confusion of voices: "*That is the whistle of the wind—it is not my voice,/ That is the fluttering of the spray*"; "*O throat! O throbbing heart!/ O all—and I singing uselessly all the night.*" Till human voices wake us, and we drown.

The aria sinks, all else continues, the boy takes over the poem, and the poet bursts from the boy. The noise level is high, even for an American poem, "The winds blowing—the notes of the wondrous bird echoing" (see that wondrous talking bird "The Raven"),/ "With angry moans the fierce old mother yet, as ever, incessantly moaning/ . . . and rustling." Gradually the noise takes form, a colloquy, a trio, bird-song, ocean-crying, boy-talk. The "undertone" (see Poe's "under-current of meaning") is the "savage old mother . . ./ To the boy's Soul's questions sullenly timing—some drowned secret hissing." But the boy is not yet ready for the secret. Suddenly he, or rather his Soul (another typical Poe device) turns to the bird with the question of questions (and now all the Poe allegory comes out into the open):

> Bird! (then said the boy's Soul,)
> Is it indeed toward your mate you sing?
>   or is it mostly to me?
> For I that was a child, my tongue's use sleeping,
> Now that I have heard you,
> Now in a moment I know what I am for—I awake,
> And already a thousand singers—a thousand songs,
>   clearer, louder, more sorrowful than yours,
> A thousand warbling echoes have started to life within me,
> Never to die.

The answer of answers is of course Whitman as American poet, and, with him, the rest of American poetry (not one singer but a thousand singers). "O you demon," Whitman continues, "singing by yourself—projecting me,/ O solitary me, listening—never more shall I cease imitating, perpetuating you." Even Poe's most famous word turns up four times in these lines, but translated from hopeless defeat to a heartfelt vow. This is the first climax of the poem.[8]

---

[8] Whitman was about twenty-six when "The Raven" was published, about thirty when Poe died. Poe's death in 1849 closely followed Whitman's first manuscript strivings (c. 1847-48) toward the new poetry.

The second climax is introduced by a curious passage about frustration. Thus far the poet has been waked, painfully, and the result is only chaos. Under such pressure, he falls apart. In a very Poesque way he apostrophizes: "O how joys, dreads, convolutions, human shapes, and all shapes, spring as from graves around me!/ O phantoms!" He talks like a man going out of his mind. He also talks like a man who fears Poe's fate, and is determined somehow to have the poetry and evade the disaster. "A word then, (for I will conquer it.)" Thus as the poem goes, we are back to diction, not word choice, vocabulary, or "poetic usage," or any other simple-minded theory of poetic diction, but "The word final, superior to all,/ Subtle, sent up." And here it comes. The time was right. The Civil War was ready to commence. And it comes all night, too, like the "Star-Spangled Banner":

> Answering, the sea,
> Delaying not, hurrying not,
> Whispered me through the night,
>   and very plainly before daybreak,
> Lisped to me constantly the low and delicious word DEATH,
> And again Death—ever Death, Death, Death,
> Hissing melodious, neither like the bird,
>   nor like my aroused child's heart,
> But edging near, as privately for me, rustling at my feet,
> And creeping thence steadily up to my ears,
> Death, Death, Death, Death, Death.

(Incidentally, or not so incidentally, there are five feet, or stresses, in a pentameter line.) "Which I do not forget," Whitman pledges himself in final recapitulation, "but fuse the song of two together." The important point is that he calls the key word precisely that, a "key" (before he had it, he called it a "clew" and demanded that it be given him; it was). "The sea whispered me." As so often in Whitman, the syntax is deliberately ambiguous. Did the sea whisper

Whitman as object (if so he's Death) or as indirect object? More likely the latter, but don't rule out the other. The drift of the passage is clear enough. American poetry had to advance from "Nevermore" to "Death," while at the same time perpetuating and honoring the "Nevermore." To find the American way of salvation, the American poet had to die to the British tradition, the British way of poetic diction, and suffer the birth pangs of a wild land noisy with natural and human dissonance and dislocation. And only an earlier American poet could see him through the agonies of death. But now it was accomplished, and American poetry would never be the same again.

From Imagism to *The Waste Land*

And when, amid no earthly moans,
Down, down that town shall settle hence,
Hell, rising from a thousand thrones,
Shall do it reverence.

Poe, "The City in the Sea"

THE THEORY or feel of American diction, like the theory of American metric and the theory of American metaphor, is seldom explicitly stated and must mostly be deduced or intuited (felt, heard) from example and practice. The easy side of it comes closest to programmatic explication (as does the theory of metric: "to compose in the sequence of the musical phrase, not in sequence of a metronome") in Ezra Pound's 1912 Imagist manifesto, the first two principles of which directly concern the language of modern, that is, American verse:

1. Direct treatment of the "thing" whether subjective or objective.
2. To use absolutely no word that does not contribute to the presentation.

Pound's theory is simple and perpetual. Under the heading "LANGUAGE," he wrote in "A Few Don'ts" (1913):

Use no superfluous word, no adjective which does not reveal something.
Don't use such an expression as "dim lands *of peace*." It dulls the image. It mixes an abstraction with the concrete. It comes

from the writer's not realizing that the natural object is always the *adequate* symbol.

Pound's best blast is probably in a January 1915 letter to Harriet Monroe, whom he was (unsuccessfully) trying to teach how to edit a literary magazine (*Poetry*). It reads as if Pound had Whitman's 1855 preface open before him, as clearly he did not; he was just a bit osmotic from dear old dad:

> Dear H.M.: ——— ——— Poetry must be *as well written as prose*. Its language must be a fine language, departing in no way from speech save by a heightened intensity (i.e. simplicity). There must be no book words, no periphrases, no inversions. . . .
>
> There must be no interjections. No words flying off to nothing. . . .
>
> There must be no cliches, set phrases, stereotyped journalese. The only escape from such is by precision, a result of concentrated attention to what [the poet] is writing. . . .
>
> Objectivity and again objectivity, and expression: no hindside-beforeness, no straddled adjectives (as "addled mosses dank"), no Tennysonianness of speech; nothing—nothing that you couldn't, in some circumstance, in the stress of some emotion, actually say. Every literaryism, every book word, fritters away a scrap of the reader's patience, a scrap of his sense of your sincerity.

The letter goes on and on, but we needn't. To the later American mind such statements ring like American copybook bravado. Evidently we are once again confronted by dialectic between the desire to speak with the perfect rectitude of proper American animals (here simply expounded, as if it were the easiest thing in the world to do) and the repressed horror of how things, including British poetry and the American language, actually jar in the ears of this country. Pound jauntily expresses the bright, brassy, progressive, pragmatic

side of the dialectic (as in Whitman's prefaces) while Eliot sorrow-
fully sings the darker side of the rape (as in Whitman's 1859 poems).
Pound rather easily eluded the domineering British tradition, where-
as Eliot had to fight out the age-old battle line after line. Pound is
the purer American poet, but Eliot speaks more directly to the real
condition of the common reader.[9]

Five minutes' reading in the *Cantos* is persuasive of at least one
point. Pound uses more languages and more kinds of the Ameri-
canized English language (he even uses British English) than any
other American poet. At worst, he is a grotesque example of Ameri-
can Eclectic, our reigning style or antistyle. (But Pound is seldom
at worst.) At best, he is a glorification of the equally American sty-
listic credo of "Right on!", or "the precise definition," *ching ming.*
(Pound has in his character much of the simple, exact, utilitarian
virtue of a great general. He often reminds me of Ulysses S. Grant.)[10]
A few lines after the opening of the Pisan *Cantos*:

[9] There are of course many millions of ways of being American. One of
the most painful and most heroic is to suffer the implications of your
identity. Not necessarily agreeing with all the ethnic implications of Pound's
analysis of himself, Eliot, and Williams, I am much struck by how accurately
it fits the poetries of the three men. In a letter to William Carlos Williams,
11 September 1920:

> There is a blood poison in America; you [i.e., Williams] can idealize the
> place (easier now that Europe is so damd shaky) all you like, but you
> haven't a drop of the cursed blood in you, and *you don't need to fight
> the disease day and night, you never have had to. Eliot has it perhaps
> worse than I have—poor devil.*

> You have the advantage of arriving in the milieu with a fresh flood of
> Europe in your veins, Spanish, French, English, Danish. You had not the
> thin milk of New York and New England from the pap; and you can
> therefore keep the environment outside you, and decently objective. (My
> emphasis.)

[10] See Pound's letter of 28 January 1935 to C. K. Ogden: "Gimme 50
more words and I can make Basic [English] into a real licherary and mule-
drivin' language, capable of blowin Freud to hell and gettin' a team from
Soap Gulch over the Hogback. You watch ole Ez do a basic Canto."

DIGENES, διγενές, but the twice crucified
                    where in history will you find it?
yet say this to the Possum: a bang, not a whimper,
        with a bang not with a whimper.

Who ever dared speak so to the Possum? And who else can speak to us so plainly? Bang vs whimper, an absolutely clear, though obviously one-sided statement of the two-faced post-Whitmanian split in American diction, the tear between the presumed limpidity of the pure American idiom (the befriended grand American expression) and the ever-present danger of relapsing into the failing mother tongue. (Failing, I mean, in its adaptability to American ends.)

The second crucifixion (following the second birth, *digenes*), which may be historical as well as personal (in "The Meter-Making Argument" I contended for two major explosions in American poetry, 1855 and 1912), is hinted at least as early as the second page of the *Cantos*, where Tiresias Theban inquires of the protagonist:

"A second time? why? man of ill star,
"Facing the sunless dead and this joyless region?"

The protagonist keeps silence, and Tiresias then prophecies the poem:

                              "Odysseus
"Shalt return through spiteful Neptune, over dark seas,
"Lose all companions."

Tiresias is not, I think, wholly distinct (as Eliot would say) from Whitman, who is perhaps not wholly distinct from Elpenor either (unless Elpenor is Eliot). However we read out the names, there is assuredly a father figure, and a wrecked poet to be memorized and placated before matters can proceed. " '*A man of no fortune, and with a name to come.*' "

Like all American poems, the poem is full of voices, learned and lewd, and Pound-poet is "poor old Homer blind, blind, as a bat,/ Ear, ear for the sea-surge, murmur of old men's voices" (canto 2), of which the voice of Henry James sounds like the first distinctly American note to disengage itself (in canto 7), "weaving an endless sentence" like the *Cantos*. In canto 3, as so often in Eliot, "the leaves are full of voices,/ A-whisper" (this *double entendre* on "leaves" is standard American equipment since Whitman; leaves are always full of voices); and canto 5 opens, "Great bulk, huge mass, thesaurus," as if the latter term were literally (it is) the substance of the epic. Topaz he manages, Pound says, "and three sorts of blue . . . Ear dull . . . Titter of sound about me, always." The result of making the American language new is promulged in canto 7 (one of the spread-the-palette cantos), where the live poet causes the husks (James, Whitman, and others) to sit at table again, "put forks in cutlets,/ And make sound like the sound of voices." ("The words rattle.") It is the same redemptive *confiteor* as in the *Pisan Cantos* (end of canto 81) where Pound admits to having "gathered from the air a live tradition/ or from a fine old eye the unconquered flame."

In the Hell cantos (14-15) we find, as we might expect, ". . . . . m/ Who disliked colloquial language," And also "the betrayers of language" with "the perverters of language." And as so frequently in the poetry of this lost land (literally England; but America is not excluded), "the air without refuge of silence,/ the drift of lice, teething,/ and above it the mouthing of orators,/ the arse-belching of preachers." The grounds for Pound's obscene assault are more than sufficiently explained in *ABC of Reading*: "Good writers are those who keep the language efficient. That is to say, keep it accurate, keep it clear. . . . Language is the main means of human communication. . . . If a nation's literature declines, the nation atrophies and decays." (As when, after the Second World War, the American news media systematically retired the precise but hateful word "capitalism" and replaced it with the meaningless twaddle of "free enterprise.") The stakes are high, the issues are simple, and the passage can be understood in as many ways as we can find successful poetic languages to illustrate it.

Beginning canto 46 Pound scoffs at the possibility that his sidekick and rival, "the Reverend Eliot/ has found a more natural language" ("you who think you will/ get through hell in a hurry"). In canto 47 he virtually recreates himself as Whitman, "That the grass grow from my body." Whitman mainly comes up—more strictly speaking, Pound goes down and back to him—in the great passage of canto 82, beginning "and the news is a long time moving/ a long time in arriving" (in *ABC of Reading*: " 'Literature is news that STAYS news' "):

> Till forty years since, Reithmuller indignant:
> "Fvy! in Tdaenmarck efen dh' beasantz gnow him,"
>   meaning Whitman, exotic, still suspect
>   four miles from Camden

With a strangly troubled allusion-quotation to "Out of the Cradle Endlessly Rocking" Pound heroically resumes and metamorphoses Whitman:

> "O troubled reflection
> "O Throat, O throbbing heart"
> How drawn, O GEA TERRA,
>   what draws as thou drawest
>   till one sink into thee by an arm's width
>   embracing thee. Drawest,
>   truly thou drawest.
> Wisdom lies next thee,
>   simply, past metaphor.

140

And then fusing "When Lilacs Last in the Dooryard Bloom'd" ("let the herbs rise in April abundant" in Pound; in Whitman "the Fourth-month"; in Eliot "the cruellest month") with the just-quoted "Out of the Cradle Endlessly Rocking," and with Whitman in general ("man, earth : two halves of the tally/ but I will come out of this know-ing no one/ neither they me . . . strong as the undertow/ of the wave receding/ but that a man should live in that further terror, and live/ the loneliness of death came upon me/ (at 3 P.M., for an instant) δακρύων [weeping],)" a man, yet by these tears a little boy again, Pound also resumes and transfigures the chthonic Hell of the American poet historically and always against the thin edge of lin-guistic and cultural death, with nothing but his own voice to fight off the primitive terror. The open road stretches further than Whitman had to imagine, further than a passage to India, all the way to the American army's death-cells at Pisa, within eye-shot of Ugolino's tower, Inferno life-size and up-to-date.

Elsewhere during an earlier stage of the same war, Eliot was writing in "Little Gidding" (*Four Quartets*) a Dantean elegy for Pound (and others) and himself. After a London air raid he en-counters "some dead master . . . a familiar compound ghost." (It must be mostly Pound. Eliot had dedicated *The Waste Land* to him under the Dantean rubric of *il miglior fabbro*. But Eliot's was "the true Dantescan voice," Pound magnanimously said, after Eliot's death: the highest compliment an American poet can pay another.) "So I assumed a double part, and cried/ And heard another's voice cry: 'What! are *you* here?'/ Although we were not." With these words Eliot recognizes his master (but does not tell us who he is). Much of Eliot's Englished *terza rima* concerns language. " 'Our concern was speech,' " says the mysterious visitor, now finding words " 'I never thought to speak/ In streets I never thought I should revisit/ When I left my body on a distant shore.' " However distant, the shore appears to be canto 1, Eliot ambiguously accepting (remem-ber he's playing a "double part"; you can't really tell which poet

141

says what), after all these years, the Tiresias-Elpenor-narrator relationship of dead poets so darkly hinted by Pound during the First World War. In 1922 Eliot was deeply in trouble, nervous, financial, and other, and Pound had hauled him out. Now it is Pound himself who is wrecked, and Eliot who is doing for Pound all he can possibly do now, homage. The *Four Quartets* is full of talk about talk, a twittering world, words reaching into silence, periphrastic studies in worn-out poetical fashions, the between-wars failure of trying to use words, "a raid on the inarticulate/ With shabby equipment," "The wave cry, the wind cry, the vast waters," the "sea howl," the "sea yelp," the whine, the wailing. "There is no end of it."

There is, however, a *media res* (we live there). Let the book fall open by chance at about mid-career, and start with "The Hollow Men" (1925), where the world ends *"not with a bang but a whimper."* American poetry is more obstetric than apocalyptic, and it is always historically real (what else could it be?):

> In this last of meeting places
> We grope together
> And avoid speech
> Gathered on this beach of the tumid river

Preliminary notes for an infernal epithalamion by Poe and Dante, equally desired and feared:

> And voices are
> In the wind's singing . . .
> Let me be no nearer
> In death's dream kingdom
> Let me also wear
> Such deliberate disguises . . .
> Behaving as the wind behaves
> No nearer—

142

Something (the Shadow) has fallen between the desire and the spasm, and as usual it appears to be the Americans' language, a torment somewhat more nihilating than anything Babbitt and H. L. Mencken had in mind:

> We are the hollow men
> We are the stuffed men
> Leaning together
> Headpiece filled with straw. Alas!
> Our dried voices, when
> We whisper together
> Are quiet and meaningless
> As wind in dry grass.

Alas, it is all one broad prairie tale from the women talking of Michelangelo (in "Prufrock"), "the voices dying with a dying fall/ Beneath the music from a farther room," the "muttering retreats," the protagonist "Full of high sentence, but a bit obtuse," "mermaids singing, each to each./ I do not think that they will sing to me" to the surf-roar colloquial feedback of Sweeney's "Fragment of an Agon":

> I gotta use words when I talk to you
> But if you understand or if you don't
> That's nothing to me and nothing to you
> We all gotta do what we gotta do
> We're gona sit here and drink this booze
> We're gona sit here and have a tune . . .

to the resigned, unspoken speech of "Marina" ("woodthrush calling through the fog"), to "the voices singing in our ears" of "Journey of the Magi," "saying/ That this was all folly/ . . . were we led all that way for/ Birth or Death? . . . no longer at ease here, in the old dispensation." Multiplication of texts can only be stopped by closing the covers of the *Collected Poems*. Early to late, Eliot's poetry is striated by the American problem of language and sound, voices, noise, and silence, "the snarled and yelping seas." We have neither youth nor age, but as it were an after dinner sleep dreaming of both; and after most dinners, a slight nightmare. Death and the Raven (Whitman and Poe) drift above, and Eliot guards the hornèd gate.

"Ash Wednesday" (1930) is a nice intermediate stopover to the whole oeuvre, which is not only religious but linguistic and cultural. Why else so stridently "renounce the voice" and "pray that I may forget/ These matters that with myself I too much discuss/ Too much explain/ Because I do not hope to turn again/ Let these words answer/ For what is done"? It is either an eternal double bind or only American history. "And God said," in good American dissenter fashion, "shall these bones live?" The bones not only live but talk, they say their say, the topic is truly endless: prophecies to the wind, chirping bones, ladies of silences, the quiet of the desert ("This is the land. We have our inheritance"), chatter of trivial things, the lost or spent word ("O my people, what have I done unto thee")—stops and steps to the mind attuned to the unworldly flowers, the volcanic dreams disgorged by the problem of poetic diction in America; elsewise, merely "distraction." Only the naive can any longer suppose that the maytime is going to be enchanted with an antique flute ("Here are the years that walk between, bearing/ Away the fiddles and the flutes").

> The silent sister veiled in white and blue
> Between the yews, behind the garden god,
> Whose flute is breathless, bent her head and sighed
>   but spoke no word . . .

The poem rides out in a crazy dialectic between the voices of Poe and Whitman, ending in thinly-veiled synthetic paradoxes:

144

> But the fountain sprang up and the bird sang down
> Redeem the time, redeem the dream
> The token of the word unheard, unspoken . . .

Internal and enveloped rhyming in the tradition of Poe, perhaps enclosing the American poetical dream:

> And the lost heart stiffens and rejoices
> In the lost lilac and the lost sea voices . . .

Whitman's voice, blend of "When Lilacs Last in the Dooryard Bloom'd" and "Out of the Cradle Endlessly Rocking." Synthetic paradoxes:

> But when the voices shaken from the yew-tree drift away
> Let the other yew be shaken and reply.

Read aloud, as it should be, "yew" is "you," shaken to reply. It is the same old quest for the hopeless word ("Not here, there is not enough silence"), through Poesque antisound ("Teach us to sit still"), ending at savage outset, "And let my cry come unto Thee." Or in Eliot's own borrowed language, "In the beginning was the Word" ("Mr. Eliot's Sunday Morning Service"). Truly, as Eliot sermonizes in "Gerontion," we are old men in a dry month being read to by boys, waiting for rain, "the word within a word," the American tone of voice within the English lexicon, "unable to speak a word," where vacant shuttles weave the wind (as in "out of the musical shuttle"). Still, we Americans shall not altogether want honor. Who, indeed, clipped the lion's wings and flea'd his rump?

Ears so tuned, we might be able to begin to listen to *The Waste Land*. First of all, be it noted that "I. The Burial of the Dead" and "V. What the Thunder Said" rhyme in an almost jocular question-and-answer way. "Dead" is shaken and replied by "said," cadavers are capped by speech. We might be able to hear the poetical character of the Americans in the "no sound of water" of the Great Dismal Swamp, and we might even be able to understand why the poet is pleased to show us "fear in a handful of dust." We will easily know why he could not speak, and his eyes failed, and he was neither living nor dead, looking into the heart of light, the silence. The dead-life, light-silence synaesthetized metaphor is the ground of the poem, and of all American poems. We might even risk a little speculation on Belladonna, the Lady of the Rocks, and Whitman's cradle-rocking crone. Tuned to the meters as to diction, we might prick up our ears when St. Mary Woolnoth keeps the hours "With a dead sound on the final stroke of nine," normally ten. ("A phenomenon which I have often noticed," Eliot slyly adds in the note to l. 68.) Indisputably we will know that the corpse Stetson plants (" ' Has it begun to sprout? Will it bloom this year?' " asks Whitman or other vocal facsimile) is next of kin to dying British poetry, and that the friendly Dog who may well dig it up again is of course, John Webster, but rather more pertinently Eliot and Edgar Allan Poe, our classic American graverobber. Ghoulishness is as native to the American poetic landscape as the mocking-bird.

"II. A Game of Chess," opens with studiedly antagonistic parodies of Shakespeare, Pope, Keats, and others, "In vials of ivory and coloured glass/ Unstoppered, lurked her strange synthetic perfumes,/ Unguent, powdered, or liquid—troubled, confused/ And drowned the sense in odours; stirred by the air/ That freshened from the window," once again the contrast between perfumes and fresh air with which Whitman set the key of "Song of Myself" and so much later American poetry. In a painting—apparently; but "as though a window gave upon the sylvan scene"—we find "the change of Philomel," the British Romantic nightingale, "by the barbarous king" (George III? Britain in general?) "so rudely forced." As a result of the rape the American poet fills all the desert with inviolable voice. And yet, historical as the rape may have been, it has always been so, and even the past-to-present tense change proves and per-petuates it:

> And still she cried, and still the world pursues,
> "Jug Jug" to dirty ears.
> And other withered stumps of time
> Were told upon the walls; staring forms
> Leaned out, leaning, hushing the room enclosed . . .

as if Poe's lover's cushion (as indeed it did) "glowed into words, then would be savagely still." Change, barbarous, forced, desert, voice, cried, forms, words, savage, still: we are now approaching the paradigmatic vocabulary of the American poetic experience (give or take half a dozen words). Still, it is not IBM statistics that most bespeak our poets but their response to "0 0 0 0 that Shake-speherian Rag." We don't mince our words, Eliot reminds us, down-shifting, "I said to her myself,/ HURRY UP PLEASE ITS TIME." Poor Albert! "He want's a good time,/ And if you don't give it him, there's others will, I said./ Oh is there, she said. Something o' that, I said./ Then I'll know who to thank, she said, and give me a straight look." (She nearly died of young George.)

"III. The Fire Sermon," opens with the flat statement: "The river's tent is broken." It is Spenser's Thames, and indeed the entire stream of British poetry. "The wind/ Crosses the brown land, unheard" (but it is going to be heard as soon as this poem gets published), "Sweet Thames, run softly, for I speak not loud or long./ But at my back in a cold blast I hear/ The rattle of the bones, and chuckle spread from ear to ear."[11] The poet muses upon the wrecks of a brother-king (Pound?) and a father-king (Whitman? Poe?), who finally fuse into *"ces voix d'enfants,"* now pretty clearly Poe and Whitman, "Jug jug jug jug jug," five to the line like "death" in "Out of the Cradle Endlessly Rocking." "So rudely forc'd" is the Whitman

[11] Native American humor.

147

bench mark (the first time Eliot used the phrase he spelled it conventionally). The Shakespeherian Rag of the typist and the small house agent's clerk " 'crept by me upon the waters,' " up—wouldn't you know it—Queen Victoria Street, Tennyson, Alfred, Lord, prop., ascensions of him hover in us yet, but not for long, while Whitman, as in Hart Crane's *The Bridge*, at junctions elegaic, wields the rebound seed, and the "Southwest wind/ Carried down stream/ The peal of bells/ White towers," until we collapse into a pleasantly snarling yelp of nearly inarticulated sound (no consonants except the half-consonantal "wah" and the liquid "l"):

> Weialala leia
> Wallala leialala

Or, as the poet unpleasantly remarks, "la la."[12]

"IV. Death by Water," is elegaic, admonitory, and, considering Whitman's death-birth by water, possibly prologue to rebirth. "V. What the Thunder Said," opens with "the frosty silence in the gardens" and the announcement that he (the British poet?) who was living is now dead, and that we (the American poets?) "who were living are now dying/ With a little patience." Patience is the emblem for the Anglo-American changeover, which slowly goes on. Again we ride out to the end (Eliot is more in the jazz tradition than any other American poet) with a mad melange of images and voices, Poe and Whitman, solo and ensemble, rock, the lack of silence, rednecks, the sound of water, the hermit-thrush, the ghostly third (see Whitman in "When Lilacs Last in the Dooryard Bloom'd" walking between the thought of death and the knowledge of death, "as with companions"), "sound high in the air," "maternal lamentation," the city that "cracks and reforms and bursts in the violet air/ Falling

---

[12] The unpleasantness is much more obvious in Eliot's public readings of the poem, or in his phonograph recording of it, than it is on the printed page.

towers," "whisper music," "Tolling reminiscent bells," and "voices singing out of empty cisterns and exhausted wells," singing grass (Whitman) over "tumbled graves" (Poe). Up close, but not quite exhausted. Out of the horror, endlessly whimpering, "the jungle crouched, humped in silence. Then spoke the thunder." The whole American put-on once more blares like trumpets as at nightfall the broken Coriolanus revives for a moment to deal the deathblow to mother culture. And then, after foreplay, the poem subtly eludes orgasm, *coitus interruptus*, the frustrated American language, and proceeds immediately to its national-international message:

> I sat upon the shore
> Fishing, with the arid plain behind me
> Shall I at least set my lands in order?

Yes. "London Bridge is falling down falling down falling down." We end in a wild spree of quotations from the *Purgatorio*, the *Pervigilium Veneris*, "*Le Prince d'Aquataine à la tour abolie*," insanity and revenge from the English "Renaissance," and into the world at large. What the Thunder Said: "Datta, Dayadhvam, Damyta [Give, Sympathize, Control]./ Shantih shantih shantih." A beleaguered American ambassador to the United Nations (beleaguered mostly by his own government) could say no more, nor better. Colonialism is dead, though it would take another world war finally to prove it, the American colonies are free of the mother country, the American Revolution, which was, after all, the first of the modern wars of national liberation, has just about run its course, and the tired, frightened voices of human nature begin to cry out against a real universe. At the end of the First World War England (and indeed all Europe) was much nearer collapse (back to proper proportions) than it knew or wanted to know; Eliot and Pound (with the equally anti-British Joyce and Yeats) emerged as the major writers of that fact. (But only Eliot won immediate fame; Pound

149

had to wait until after the Second World War.) As I have said, there is no real conclusion to *The Waste Land* because there is no final solution of the linguistic problem engendered by four centuries of highly questionable Westward Movements. (Movements in other directions too.) Returned from the printed page to real life, the Sanskrit word "shantih" translates "to be continued and perhaps one day concluded." Lucifer is still in harness, though with ever increasing freedom of movement, but a notable shifting of forces has taken place. "Troy [London, Western Europe, the world] but a heap of smouldering boundary stones" (canto 4). Down, down, it settles, while a couple of ordinary Midwesterners, having no political power, but only the gift of tongues, mainly their poetic loyalty to the American vernacular, rise from a pair of Hell-soaked thrones to do it reverence.

Linguistic Lapses in Crane and Stevens

Come forth, sweet democratic despots of the west!

WHITMAN, *Democratic Vistas*

SOME DO and some don't. As we have just seen three times—
Whitman, Pound, Eliot—the American poet can at his best live with
his linguistic problem, and he can even make great poetic capital out
of his suffering. What seems to be common to all three poets, in
other ways so disparate, is a deep humility toward their medium,
an ear firmly gripped by the sound of the English language in Ameri-
ca, and, conversely, gripping it. That much presupposed, the poet
is free to ramble far and wide, even to the extent of Pound's drag-
ging in as many foreign languages as he knows or dabbles in, which
is quite a few. But in the age preceding Whitman, when such a re-
lationship to the national idiom was not yet firmly established—as it
was not in Bryant, Emerson, or Lowell, Poe being a marginal case—
the poetry comes out effete, troubled, and ineffectual. After Whit-
man, approximately the same phenomenon tends to recur during
periods of strong conservative reassertion. Poets like Hart Crane and
Wallace Stevens dislocate themselves, or find themselves dislocated,
from the radical tradition of American poetry, with its realistic em-
phasis on the spoken language, and, lacking any other way out of
their Anglo-American dilemma, they tie themselves up in knots.
And the more intensely they write, the more the knots tighten. How-
ever different the poetic results in the two men, the underlying prob-
lem is essentially the same: overlooking the complete relativity of
all language and poetry and indeed of all human experience, they
will be satisfied with nothing less than an Absolute—an absolute
word, an absolute poem. Since no such things exist in nature, or

151

could exist in nature, unless or until nature itself ceases to exist, the poetry tends to drift away from the human condition, which is ineradicably particular and linguistic, and it consequently fails to achieve the poetic merit we might have expected from two such prodigious talents.

Partly because he died so young, partly because he lacked Stevens' philosophical complications, Crane is somewhat easier to figure out. In simplest terms, he wants a linguistic base, a poetic language, a poetic diction, and consequently he never writes a poem all the way through, but only in bits and starts. Like Emerson and Emily Dickinson, he is at his best in the single line or pair of lines. Every lover of Crane will have his own favorites, but here are some examples I think no one will wish to quarrel with:

The bottom of the sea is cruel. ("Voyages, I")

Permit me voyage, love, into your hands . . . ("Voyages, III")

In all the argosy of your bright hair I dreamed
Nothing so flagless as this piracy. ("Voyages, V")

My trespass vision shrinks to face his wrong. ("The Idiot")

Of course every poet is entitled to brilliant lines, but what is of chief significance in Crane is that these brilliant lines are so much better than the poems of which they ostensibly form a part. And this atomism goes even further, down to the single word. In each of these lines a single word, or a paired word, carries the poetic payload: "cruel," "voyage," "argosy-flagless," and "trespass."

At his simplest, Crane can write with absolute perfection, as in the final stanza of "Praise for an Urn":

> Scatter these well-meant idioms
> Into the smoky spring that fills
> The suburbs, where they will be lost.
> They are no trophies of the sun.

Here no one word obtrudes—"trophies" may at first sound like an exception, but it finally settles into place—and the whole passage demonstrates that desirable esemplastic poetical power of which Coleridge so imaginatively spoke. Crane rarely possesses it. Despite his yearnings to be a new Whitman, he is in fact a recycled Emerson-Dickinson. Even when he is trying to be plain and easy, Crane's inherited commitments usually trip him up, as in the opening stanza of "To Brooklyn Bridge":

> How many dawns, chill from his rippling rest
> The seagull's wings shall dip and pivot him,
> Shedding white rings of tumult, building high
> Over the chained bay waters Liberty—

It starts smoothly enough, but then that word "tumult" slaps the reader in the face, the old Emerson trick of impounding a metaphor in a single surprising word. The ending of the stanza—the abstract polysyllable with an "ee" sound (Immortality, Eternity, etc.)—is pure cop-out Dickinson, here complete with a capital letter and a dash. Most of the time Crane tries too hard in the wrong direction (American conservatives are often overintense); instead of letting the genius of the language lead and instruct him, he vents his rhetorical passions on it, and naturally the vocabulary falls apart:

> O Thou steeled Cognizance whose leap commits
> The agile precincts of the lark's return;
> Within whose lariat sweep encinctured sing
> In single chrysalis the many twain,—
> Of stars Thou art the stitch and stallion glow
> And like an organ, Thou, with sound of doom—
> Sight, sound and flesh Thou leadest from time's realm
> As love strikes clear direction for the helm.

Crane is not, as so many people used to think, the avant-garde of modern poetry, but a retrogression to, and exasperation of, certain

153

aspects of American poetic diction that were clear at least as early as Emerson. In its exaggerated mixture of metaphors, it sounds like a British poem run mad. Unlike a British poem, it has no keeping, it is not checked by unity of tone, by poetic diction. The lines just quoted are nominalistic to the point of nearly total obscurity and bombast. And just what is all that obscurity and bombast about? A bridge.

This perpetual Emersonian metaphorical fussing with the single word, this over-strained mixing of metaphors in the British mode, Crane called "the logic of metaphor," a pretentious phrase concealing the truth that Crane had no poetic language to work with. At the other extreme, Crane was religiously in love with the "unfractioned idiom" of the Pure Logos, and this passion equally led him away from poetry. In "General Aims and Theories," he made as clear as he could this second goal: "It is as though a poem gave the reader as he left it a single, new *word*, never before spoken and impossible to actually enunciate, but self-evident as an active principle in the reader's consciousness henceforward." This is really confounded confusion. A poem is formed of words. It is not and can never be *a* word. It can have a single constituting metaphor, and it may be that Crane in this passage is groping toward that conception. Given Crane's propensities, however, it is more likely that he means, or thinks he means, just what he says.

Thematically, Crane's poetry rarely and glancingly confronts the real issues of American poetic diction, but it almost never drives these issues to a satisfactory conclusion. In *The Bridge* Columbus-Crane finds himself "between two worlds," where "This third, of water, tests the word," and "Some inmost sob, half-heard, dissuades the abyss,/ Merges the wind in measure to the waves"; still, the invocation more or less ends with the "sounding heel" of Elohim, which is not, if one may say so, much of a sound. Again, in "The River," the various sounds ("the din and slogans of the year"— Crane's marginal prose direction wearily reminds us once more of his fundamental disjunction from American popular speech) culminate in "Dead echoes!" And even at the end when Crane tries to resuscitate the American Dream (but only to "spend" it) as the Mississippi River, we come to climax, not in the particular American literary situation, but in a highly rhetorical universal Passion, which speaks in "wide tongues" and then "hosannas silently"; that is, it does not speak at all, it celebrates.

"Cape Hatteras" ("a kind of ode to Whitman") reveals how close Crane came to sensing the nature of the American poetic problem and why it was impossible for him really to grapple with it: blithely disregarding the inherent dialectic and pluralism of the American poetic enterprise, Crane wants us, and our poets, bound and "throbbing with one voice." Whitman would have been shocked by this. He wanted thousands of American poets, all different, and he did not want to be imitated. Earlier in the same section, Crane had imagined himself "Where strange tongues vary messages of surf," which *is* good Whitman, and nationally reasonable; there are pleasant lines recalling "Out of the Cradle Endlessly Rocking"; and there is a curious passage about birds (raven, condor, albatross) which may imply that Whitman surpassed Poe and Coleridge, thereby transcending both the American and the British Romantic traditions. But none of this is very certain. The certainty is that Crane's mind is always being blown by static or other unwanted noise: "Man hears himself an engine in a cloud!" Naturally he doesn't like it. Naturally the poetry falls apart. Crane's apostrophe to Emily Dickinson (his genuine poetic mom and a bad influence), "transmuting silence with that stilly note/ Of pain," is bad sentimental poetry, and probably worse than anything she ever wrote. His overwrought apostrophe to Poe is in the last analysis only a self-centered invitation to hell and death. *The Bridge* increasingly gives itself away in such lines as "Our tongues recant like beaten weather vanes," and "I counted the echoes assembling, one after one." That would make at least two, but Crane cannot tolerate pluralities. Everything in his poetry culminates in an Absolute One, customarily White, which would seem a virtual impossibility after Melville; but Crane was a lifelong devotee of the impossible. "One Song, one Bridge of Fire!" Little wonder that he finally had to ask "Thy pardon for this history, whitest Flower,/ O Answerer of all." Years later, in one of his most moving and most troubled poems, "The Broken Tower," Crane wrote:

> And so it was I entered the broken world
> To trace the visionary company of love, its voice
> An instant in the wind (I know not whither hurled)
> But not for long to hold each desperate choice.
>
> My word I poured. But was it cognate . . . ?

Cognate with God, Crane presumably means, the Holy Spirit who spoke through the prophets, not through the poets. Crane never understood that there is no one voice, American or other, but as many voices as there are people. The relevant question is whether Crane's language was cognate with the realities of the American poetic situation. With many reservations and dubieties, and with many unreserved admirations and affections, the answer, at least for this particular occasion, has to be no. It is the all but inevitable answer to the kind of poet whose best line reads: "The earth may glide diaphanous to death."

"For some of us, Wallace Stevens is America's chief conjurer—as bold a virtuoso and one with as cunning a rhetoric as we have produced. . . . His repercussive harmonics . . . suggest a linguist creating several languages within a single language. . . . But best of all, the bravura. Upon the general marine volume of statement is set a parachute-spinnaker of verbiage which looms out like half a cantaloupe and gives the body of the theme the air of a fabled argosy advancing. Not infrequently Wallace Stevens' 'noble accents and lucid, inescapable rhythms' point to the universal parent, Shake-

156

speare." That was Marianne Moore speaking, in "Conjuries that Endure" (1937), uncharacteristically carried away by the sound of her own voice, or perhaps by Stevens' voice. Miss Moore is a hard person to tangle with. Still, she wrote in 1937; a lot of marine volume has slipped away underfoot since then; and surely it is an open question whether conjuries can endure, however cunning, virtuoso, and bravura.

Stevens talked a lot about poetry, sometimes well, sometimes ill, and he needs to be listened to, though not necessarily agreed with. Probably the center of Stevens poetical problem lies in a single confessional sentence he wrote in "Adagia": "Life is an affair of people not of places. But for me life is an affair of places and that is the trouble." That is indeed a trouble, for places have no language except that of the people who live in them. From the beginning Stevens was dislocated from his proper medium, and he knew it. A few sentences after that sentence we find another one in which Stevens sounds like he is trying to sound like William Carlos Williams: "The loss of a language creates confusion or dumbness." A few pages later we find an attempt to thrust out of this situation, ending in total confusion:

Every poem is a poem within a poem: the poem of the idea within the poem of the words.

Poetry is the gaiety (joy) of language.

Words are everything else in the world.

When poetry and language are set in such total antithesis, something is clearly wrong. (Yet three pages earlier Stevens had said: "Words are the only melodeon.")

From the letters and prose it is obvious that Stevens spent a lot of time agonizing about his liabilities and a lot of time trying to bluff

157

his way out of them. One of his strongest tacks was "gaiety" (never, I think, very well defined). Referring to "The Emperor of Ice-Cream," Stevens wrote William Rose Benét (6 January 1933) about "the essential gaudiness of poetry." In "Imagination as Value" he said flat out that "we know that in poetry bigness and gaiety are precious characteristics of the diction." And in the "Adagia," "Gaiety in poetry is a precious characteristic but it should be a characteristic of diction." Stevens is clearly trying to hold onto his intellectual integrity. Still, it is equally clear that the gaiety game can never work. However phrased, it always divorces the medium (words, words, words) from the product (the poem).

Although Stevens saw his way to say provocatively (as long ago quoted) that "nothing could be more inappropriate to American literature than its English source since the Americans are not British in sensibility," he was never able to match that *aperçu* about literature and sensibility with a comparable *aperçu* about language. Stevens' second tack was to come about and beat his way to weather toward France. "A good many words come to me from French origins. I think we have a special relation to French and even that it can be said that English and French are a single language" (letter of 21 November 1950). In the "Adagia," "French and English constitute a single language." Any Frenchman could have straightened Stevens out on that point, though Stevens would probably have gone right on stubbornly persisting in his giant overstatement and confusion. It was necessary to justify his own Francophile virtuosity and to cover up the gaping wound of his disjunction from American common speech. Ultimately Stevens built a huge parachute-spinnaker of verbiage out of all this philological nonsense, and for a while this half a cantaloupe seemed to keep his yacht billowing happily downwind:

> The prejudice in favor of plain English, for instance, comes to nothing. I have never been able to see why what is called Anglo-Saxon should have the right to higgle and haggle all over the

page, contesting the right of other words. If a poem seems to require a hierophantic phrase, the phrase should pass. This is a way of saying that one of the consequences of the ordination of style is not to limit it, but to enlarge it, not to impoverish it, but to enrich and liberate it. ("Two or Three Ideas")

Unfortunately for Stevens' argument, liberation is not the issue. The issue is the organic relevance of the "ornaments," as Whitman had long since pointed out.

Stevens' last tack, and his worst, was to fall back on a kind of plutocratic solipsism. In a letter of 17 February 1955 he was writing: "Every poet's language is his own distinct tongue. He cannot speak the common language and continue to write poetry any more than he can think the common thought and continue to be a poet. It is not a matter of a great difference but just of a difference." Precisely. Just where do you draw the line between a great difference and a difference? If Stevens is saying that every poet has his own voice and should avoid banality, he is of course correct, though not very original. But as usual Stevens seems to be hinting at something more. "He cannot speak the common language." If not, how can he purify the language of the tribe? "Any more than he can think the common thought." If not, then to whom is he speaking? More drastically, who speaks? These are not easy questions to answer. What is easy to sense is that the conservative reassertion is out of control. Stevens has moved 180° away from Pound's lucid demand that "Poetry must be *as well written as prose*. Its language must be a fine language, departing in no way from speech save by a heightened intensity (i.e. simplicity). There must be no book words, etc."

Stevens' poetry shows a slow agonized "development" from early gaiety to late abstraction and coldness. The split is evident from the very beginning, as in "The Emperor of Ice-Cream," which is a drawn battle between what pretends to be a very gritty reality (but is, in

159

fact, somewhat Platonic) and a gaudy impertinence. Here are the couplet endings of the two stanzas:

> Let be be finale of seem.
> The only emperor is the emperor of ice-cream.
>
> Let the lamp affix its beam.
> The only emperor is the emperor of ice-cream.

The first thing that strikes the ear is the metrical antitheses. In the first line, seven or eight tight, tough syllables, in which nearly every syllable is working; in the second line, fourteen syllables, most of which are not working at all. On a closer look, the split in diction is even more striking. In each pair, the first line demands some kind of absolute reality, while the second line contradicts that reality with a kind of confectionary linguistic irresponsibility. However often explicated and excused, "The only emperor is the emperor of ice-cream" is not only a silly remark but ultimately a meaningless one. These are the two extremes of Stevens' poetry, and even the titles tell the tale. "The Paltry Nude Starts on a Spring Voyage" is a typical early title. The last title in the *Collected Poems* is "Not Ideas about the Thing but the Thing Itself."

There are many superficial charms in the gaiety of the early poems, and there are, for some people, many fascinating metaphysical puzzles, but very little poetry, in the late ones. It seems obvious that the Stevens who will endure is a kind of middle-ground Stevens, mostly early, but not entirely, which is equally distant from the two extremes—neither the Stevens of "Sea Surface Full of Clouds" nor the Stevens of "Notes toward a Supreme Fiction"—the human but reserved Stevens of such poems as "Sunday Morning" or "The Idea of Order at Key West." In these poems we find neither frou-frou French impressionism nor mangled metaphysics, but a simple yet elevated diction that bestows dignity on the commonest

160

objects and situations. Or to take an example from a poem not yet cited, the final stanza of "Le Monocle de Mon Oncle" (the title is gaudy, and the poem deliberately starts gaudy, but it doesn't end that way):

> A blue pigeon it is, that circles the blue sky,
> On sidelong wing, around and round and round.
> A white pigeon it is, that flutters to the ground,
> Grown tired of flight. Like a dark rabbi, I
> Observed, when young, the nature of mankind,
> In lordly study. Every day, I found
> Man proved a gobbet in my mincing world.
> Like a rose rabbi, later, I pursued,
> And still pursue, the origin and course
> Of love, but until now I never knew
> That fluttering things have so distinct a shade.

That is not the American vernacular, but it is close enough to the vernacular to be poetically viable. The basic form of the verse is prose structure of a rather discursive, thoughtful, even scholarly type, against which Stevens plays the full brilliance of his gift for the special word, for internal and end rhyming, together with a total control of the meter, perfect modern American iambic pentameter, and yet demonstrably related to the British tradition, which delivers each syllable at the right time and place with its proper poetic valence. Here is American conservative poetry at its finest, and it deserves long and close attention by the serious reader. Why, for example, is that final word "shade" so perfectly right? Because it does not rhyme, except aslant, very aslant, with "pursued," which picks up the "blue-pursue-knew" rhyme scheme running through the stanza? Or because ultimately it does rhyme with the fluttering word on sidelong wing which haunts the stanza, and which Stevens in his supreme artistry will not let us have, namely the word "made"?

161

That is the true and final word of the poem, and it is given us only indirectly and by inference in the last sound, in which the poem is truly and finally made.

Stevens' late poetry will be higgled and haggled about all over the critical lot for some time to come, though the ultimate result is already predetermined by the nature of the poetry. One simple fact about it is immediately clear, and for present purposes, sufficient. Stevens is driving toward an absolute poetry which is pseudo-religious in nature and which, if it could succeed, as of course it never can, would leave both God and poetry undone. Insofar as he proceeds toward this goal, Stevens dismantles his own poetry. It is not a matter to argue about. Every reader must respond with his own ear. My own ear is offended even by the titles of such poems as "*Esthétique du Mal*" (as we have seen, Stevens was no great shakes at aesthetics, and he was even more inept at epistemology and ontology). Predictably the poetry comes out flat as prose:

> One might have thought of sight, but who could think
> Of what it sees, for all the ill it sees?
> Speech found the ear, for all the evil sound,
> But the dark italics it could not propound.
> And out of what one sees and hears and out
> Of what one feels, who could have thought to make
> So many selves, so many sensuous worlds,
> As if the air, the mid-day air, was swarming
> With the metaphysical changes that occur,
> Merely in living as and where we live.

In "The Irrational Element in Poetry," Stevens revealingly wrote: "We say that we perfect diction. We simply grow tired." Some of us also grow callous, both about our language and about other people. In the same poem we find this kind of linguistic-moral disaster:

162

Life is a bitter aspic. We are not
At the centre of a diamond. At dawn,
The paratroopers fall and as they fall
They mow the lawn. A vessel sinks in waves
Of people, as big bell-billows from its bell
Bell-bellow in the village steeple. Violets,
Great tufts, spring up from buried houses
Of poor, dishonest people, for whom the steeple,
Long since, rang out farewell, farewell, farewell.

The gaudiness of the diction cannot forever conceal the fact that Stevens is saying virtually nothing except that poor people are dishonest, a poetic linkage impossible either to understand or to admire. It is true that as he grew older, Stevens also grew more politically conservative. But I do not think the badness of the poetry is a simple correlative of the political conservatism. The underlying cause of Stevens' decline is his increasing insensitivity to the way other people speak. Even if it is also a problem of politics and morals, it is first of all a problem of poetic diction.

"Notes toward a Supreme Fiction" ("It Must be Abstract," "It Must Change," "It Must Give Pleasure") displays a worsening lapse, and is as far as I care to follow Stevens' poetic disintegration. We have now arrived at this kind of poetry (not poetry at all; bad prose; bad metaphysics too):

Phoebus is dead, ephebe. But Phoebus was
A name for something that never could be named.
There was a project for the sun and is.

There is a project for the sun. The sun
Must bear no name, gold flourisher, but be
In the difficulty of what it is to be.

Naturally the poem is full of confusion about language:

> He [the poet] tries by a peculiar speech to speak
>
> The peculiar potency of the general,
> To compound the imagination's Latin with
> The lingua franca et jocundissima.

But the language Stevens uses in these lines is precisely the reverse of the kind of language he claims the poet is trying for. And of course the confusion about language is caused by absolutism:

> To find the real,
> To be stripped of every fiction except one,
>
> The fiction of an absolute—Angel,
> Be silent in your luminous cloud and hear
> The luminous melody of proper sound.

But as anyone with even the slightest ear will be aware by now, there is in this poetry no proper sound at all.

"Notes Toward a Supreme Fiction" ends with a coda in which Stevens tries to associate himself with the World War Two American soldier:

> The soldier is poor without the poet's lines,
>
> His pretty syllabi, the sounds that stick,
> Inevitably modulating, in the blood.
> And war for war, each has its gallant kind.
>
> How simply the fictive hero becomes the real;
> How gladly with proper words the soldier dies,
> If he must, or lives on the bread of faithful speech.

164

The poet is poor (or even dead) without the soldier's life, as Stevens might have remembered had he taken any real interest in what he was saying. As we have seen, since the time of Whitman, war has been an available constituting metaphor for American poetry. But what a comedown from Whitman's starkly suffering war poems to such bravura conjuries! Did Stevens really suppose that men who survived Coral Sea and the Battle of the Bulge would respond to a poetry so remote from and so insensitive to their real pain? From time immemorial, soldiers have had a language of their own, a highly charged sub-variant of the American (or whatever) vernacular, and it is a lot hotter than anything Stevens ever cooked up. Except on a few truly noble occasions, Stevens failed to keep faith with the American vernacular and in the long run the ongoing American vernacular will reduce him to the status of a minor poet. "Surely for millions of men and women," Stevens said, "the act of joining the armed forces is measurably a poetic act." Major poets simply don't talk like that.

William Carlos Williams, M.D.

> Let
> me out! (Well, go!) this rhetoric
> is real!
>
> WILLIAMS, Paterson

"AND WAR FOR WAR, each has its gallant kind" (Stevens). True, but Williams, our most diligent self-appointed inspector of linguistic snow-jobs, would naturally view the matter from a different angle:

> How shall I find examples? Some boy
> who drove a bull-dozer through
> the barrage at Iwo Jima and turned it
> and drove back making a path for the others—
>
>   Voiceless, his
> action gracing a flame
>
>   —but lost, lost
> because there is no way to link
> the syllables anew to imprison him
>
>   No twist of the flame
> in his own image   :   he goes nameless
> until a Niké shall live in his honor—
>
> And for that, invention is lacking,
> the words are lacking:
>
>   the waterfall of the
> flames, a cataract reversed, shooting
> upward (what difference does it make?)

The language,

> Beautiful thing—that I
> make a fool of myself, mourning the lack
> of dedication
>
>   mourning its losses
>
> for you

There is American diction at its finest, mourning its losses, for you, out of absence carving a Niké that can live in our actual conditions. There is also the best of Williams, and all we have to do is comb it out.

The epigraph concludes one of myriad passages in *Paterson* wherein the poet attempts to articulate the mindless roar of the Passaic River and Falls, the mindless roar of all immediate prelinguistic experience:

> The past above, the future below
> and the present pouring down: the roar,
> the roar of the present, a speech—
> is, of necessity, my sole concern . . . .
>
>   I must
> find my meaning and lay it, white,
> beside the sliding water: myself—
> comb out the language— . . .

The combing metaphor—as in combing out a wet dog poet—appears elsewhere in the poem, and is obviously critical to the issue of discriminating kinds of verbal communication (or lack of it):

> (What common language to unravel?
>   . . combed into straight lines
> from that rafter of a rock's
> lip.)

167

(Pun on "lines," for Williams is nearly as obsessed with metric as with diction.)

Like all his compeers in the radical tradition, Williams tends toward a pro-American, anti-English linguistic bias:

> We poets have to talk in a language which is not English. It is the American idiom. Rhythmically it's organized as a sample of the American idiom. It has as much originality as jazz.

But Williams very quickly transcends this dilemma with the further realization that the escape from the British tradition into the American vernacular in and of itself solves no problems but rather creates them. The American idiom is quite as uncommunicative as Palgrave's *Golden Treasury*, until the new poet has at it:

Voices!

multiple and inarticulate . voices
clattering loudly to the sun, to
the clouds. Voices!
assaulting the air gaily from all sides.

—among which the ear strains to catch
the movement of one voice among the rest
—a reed-like voice

of peculiar accent

This is Sunday in the park, with the commingled voices of the Falls, the people, and the poet:

the voice
that has ineluctably called them—

that unmoving roar! . . .

—his voice, one among many (unheard)
moving under all . . .

                   from place
to place he moves,
his voice mingling with other voices
—the voice in his voice
opening his old throat, blowing out his lips,
kindling his mind (more
than his mind will kindle)

If the poet wants "loveliness and/ authority in the world," he must hear it in the voices of real people, including himself, and get it straight on the page. And everything seems to conspire against him.

In Williams' world, there is only one certainty, but it suffices. "Words are the burden of poems, poems are made of words." From that sound proposition flows a Manichean division:

A false language. A true. A false language pouring—a language (misunderstood) pouring (misinterpreted) without dignity . . .

The true language is of course American poetry still struggling to be born. "I have much to say to you . . . and I am aware of the stream/ that has no language." Most of the time the birth seems only an impossible dream, "so close are we to ruin every day," except in the obvious fact that the despair is, of course, *Paterson* page after page coming to birth. "The language is missing them/ they die also/ incommunicado." Divorce and noncommunication are the villains of the epic. Whether you shriek and fall with Mrs. Cumming or leap with Sam Patch ("Speech had failed him. He was confused. The world had been drained of its meaning"), you make

169

only the difference between "a body found next spring/ frozen in an ice-cake; or a body/ fished next day from the muddy swirl—/ both silent, uncommunicative." The genteel lady and the heroic poet come to the same thing:

> Death lies in wait,
> a kindly brother—
> full of the missing words,
> the words that never get said—
> a kindly brother to the poor.

But death is not so kindly a brother to the young:

> Old newspaper files,
> to find—a child burned in a field,
> no language. Tried, aflame, to crawl under
> a fence to go home. So be it. Two others,
> boy and girl, clasped in each others' arms
> (clasped also by the water) So be it. Drowned
> wordless in the canal. So be it.

So be it, indeed. "Haven't you forgot your virgin purpose,/ the language?" the poet is always (and not superfluously) asking himself, and usually getting a question for an answer, "What language?"

Book Three, says the author's headnote, "will seek a language to make them [the modern replicas] vocal," but how this is to be encompassed is not entirely clear, or certainly not easy, for the language itself, reeling from divorce, "stutters." Difficulties endlessly proliferate. "A marriage riddle:/ So much talk of the language— when there are no/ ears." Or to take a more complex example, which drives through difficulty toward the beginnings of expression:

> The language   .   words
> without style! whose scholars (there are none)
> or dangling, about whom

the water weaves its strands encasing them
in a sort of thick lacquer, lodged
under its flow   .

Caught (in mind)
beside the water he looks down, listens!
But discovers, still, no syllable in the confused
uproar: missing the sense (though he tries)
untaught but listening, shakes with the intensity
of his listening   .

The most moving passages are dialectical between the poet and
"Beautiful thing," the oriented goal of all poetry:

Go home. Write. Compose   .

Ha!

Be reconciled, poet, with your world, it is
the only truth!

Ha!

—the language is worn out.

And She   —
You have abandoned me!

Still, we always move toward parturition, sometimes Christ-like:

Peter Brueghel, the elder, painted
a Nativity, painted a Baby
new born!
among the words.

171

Pediatrician-poet-lover-father Williams admonishes himself to go and do likewise:

> Paterson,
>> keep your pecker up
>>> whatever the detail!
>>>> Anywhere is everywhere:
>> You can learn from poems
>>> that an empty head tapped on
>>>> sounds hollow
>> in any language! The figures
>>> are of heroic size.

Other times he is more lightly amorous, "Let the words/ fall any way at all—that they may/ hit love aslant. It will be a rare/ visitation." Ultimately, of course, nothing but the best—American best, that is—will suffice:

> Sing me a song to make death tolerable, a song
> of a man and a woman: the riddle of a man
> and a woman.
>> What language could allay our thirsts,
> what winds lift us, what floods bear us
>>>> past defeats
>> but song but deathless song?

We appear to have rounded back to British Romantic poetry, but with a certain difference. This is democratic poetry, and like all democratic poetry the deathless song is not so much for the poet as for the people, who also appear in it. Typically, they appear as voices (roar; noise; silences; colloquial nonsense). "He," the poet, "hears! Voices   .   indeterminate." He must determine them. *"What do I do? I listen, to the water falling. . . . This is my entire occupation."*

172

And the occupation is forever and unremitting:

Who am I?

—the voice!

—the voice rises, neglected
(with its new) the unfaltering
language. Is there no release?

Give it up. Quit it. Stop writing.

For common man as for poet, there is no release short of death. Against divorce and noncommunication, which is already death, stand birth and birth's poetic analogue:

Without invention nothing is well spaced,
unless the mind change, unless
the stars are new measured, according
to their relative positions, the
line will not change, the necessity
will not matriculate: unless there is
a new mind there cannot be a new
line, the old will go on
repeating itself with recurring
deadliness: . . .

without invention the line
will never again take on its ancient
divisions when the word, a supple word,
lived in it, crumbled now to chalk.

We have certainly rounded back to the meter-making argument, though it is a nice question whether Williams' concern for metric encloses his concern for diction (lines are made of words) or the other way around (words drive lines into being). It makes no matter.

> We know nothing and can know nothing   .
>   but
> the dance, to dance to a measure
> contrapuntally,
>   Satyrically, the tragic foot.

American poetry is not always satire or tragedy, of course, though it is always difficulty. In the great poets like Williams it is difficulty met head-on and mastered:

> She did not want to live to be
>
> an old woman to wear a china doorknob
> in her vagina to hold her womb up—but
>
> she came to that, resourceful, what?

American poetry seldom gets much better than that. The lines are new and ancient (the last two even rhyme), the words are supple and alive. The voice is heard. The rhetoric is real.

The reality comes from Williams' personal and poetic realization that people and language, babies and words, are the same thing. Many a previous American poet had sensed as much, but perhaps it took a poet who was a doctor to spell it out for us. Thus Williams writes of the poetic process in his *Autobiography* (1951):

> Do we not see that we are inarticulate? That is what defeats us. It is our inability to communicate to another how we are locked within ourselves, unable to say the simplest thing of importance to one another, any of us, even the most valuable, that

makes our lives like those of a litter of kittens in a wood-pile. That gives the physician, and I don't mean the high-priced psychoanalyst, his opportunity. . . .

The physician enjoys a wonderful opportunity actually to witness the words being born. Their actual colors and shapes are laid before him carrying their tiny burdens which he is privileged to take into his care with their unspoiled newness. He may see the difficulty with which they have been born and what they are destined to do. No one else is present but the speaker and ourselves, we have been the words' very parents. Nothing is more moving.

Later, things get more complicated. All of us, Williams' patients, grow accustomed to "the range of communication which is likely to reach us," and not much of it does. Still, our stale language contains our poem, the undercurrent of the poem of our actually lived lives. And that is why the poet listens.

The poem springs from the half-spoken words of such patients as the physician sees from day to day. He observes it in the peculiar, actual conformations in which its life is hid. Humbly he presents himself before it and by long practice he strives as best he can to interpret the manner of its speech. In that the secret lies. This, in the end, comes perhaps to be the occupation of the physician after a lifetime of careful listening.

It all makes good sense. America is and has always been an ailing nation. Not in a Bohemian garret, but in a military hospital or a doctor's office is where America can be heard and healed.

Whitman and Williams are far and away the most loveable of American poets, and it is now easy to see why. Whitman gave the best years of his life to the wounded and dying soldiers, many of them still boys, of the Civil War. Williams spent his life caring for expectant mothers, delivering babies, and watching over the development of small children. Whitman was called to death, Williams to birth, but as we know death and birth are very closely related in the politics of American poetry. What both men equally derived from their experience was a knowledgeable concern for human beings in extremis, and an ability to get that concern into form and language, a concern which seems to be virtually the positive definition of that poetry. Any of our poets can say—and most of them sooner or later get around to saying it—that the American language is not quite the English language. Nobody but Williams can say it like this (still from the *Autobiography*):

> At City College, New York . . . I was defining our right as Americans to our own language, saying that English, its development from Shakespeare's day to this, does not primarily concern us. [That, as we have seen, is not the whole truth.]
>
> "But this language of yours," said one of the instructors, himself an obvious Britisher, "where does it come from?"
>
> "From the mouths of Polish mothers," I replied.

Poe Against the Thin Edge

> Poe stayed against the thin edge, driven to be heard by the
> battering racket about him to a distant screaming—the pure
> essence of his locality.
>
> WILLIAMS, *In the American Grain*

TWO SENTENCES after that sentence about Poe, Williams gives
us a brief but moving historical image of Lincoln "walking up and
down in Springfield on the narrow walk between the two houses,
day after day, with a neighbor's baby, borrowed for the occasion,
sleeping inside his cape upon his shoulder to give him stability while
thinking and composing his coming speeches." Williams is a cun-
ning master of juxtapositions. Poe, the great Southerner, childless,
who inspired Whitman into the birth of death, and thus of Ameri-
can poetry; Lincoln, the great Northerner, our first assassinated
President, with a borrowed baby on his shoulder to give him sta-
bility. There is much agony in American poetry as well as in Amer-
ican politics. Williams clearly senses the interrelatedness.

The necessity of discriminating, or even alienating, the American
from the English language, and the near impossibility of doing so:
that contradiction doubtless accounts for the alternating wails and
silences of our national poetry. The contradiction is clearest in Poe,
though of all the major American poets Poe seems least consciously
aware of the contradiction. That anomaly, also, Williams under-
stood:

> On him is FOUNDED A LITERATURE—typical; an anger to sweep
> out the unoriginal, that became ill-tempered, a monomaniacal
> driving to destroy, to annihilate the copied, the slavish, the FALSE
> literature about him: this is the major impulse in his notes—

177

darkening as he goes, losing the battle, as he feels himself going under—he emerges as the ghoulish, the driven back. It is the crudeness with which he was attacked in his own person, scoffed at—

Or again:

It is only in the conception of a *possibility* that he is most distinguished. His greatness is in that he turned his back and faced inland, to originality, with the identical gesture of a Boone. [Also with the identical gesture of the hero of *Paterson*.]

And for *that* reason he is unrecognized. Americans have never recognized themselves. How can they? It is impossible until someone invent the ORIGINAL terms. As long as we are content to be called by somebody else's terms, we are incapable of being anything but our own dupes.

Thus Poe must suffer by his originality. Invent that which is new, even if it be made of pine from your own yard, and there's none to know what you have done. It is because there's no *name*. This is the cause of Poe's lack of recognition. He was American.

Poe as the conception of the possibility of American poetry is the only possible ending of this book. Sweet Thames . . .

In "The City in the Sea," the city sinks "amid no earthly moans." At the end of "The Sleeper," the dead woman, seen as a child, idly throws stones against a family sepulchre, "remote, alone," and thinks (thought), "poor child of sin," she forced an echo from "the dead who groaned within." In "The Coliseum," echoes and " 'prophetic sounds and loud' " arise forever from ruin, " 'As melody from Memnon to the Sun.' " (Son?) America in Poe is always ruined, moaning, sounding, or silent. In "To One in Paradise," Poe curiously writes:

178

For, alas! alas! with me
   The light of Life is o'er!
   No more—no more—no more—
(Such language holds the solemn sea
   To the sands upon the shore)
Shall bloom the thunder-blasted tree,
   Or the stricken eagle soar!

These lines flow in a divided stream into "The Raven" and into "Out of the Cradle Endlessly Rocking" (once entitled "A Word Out of the Sea"). Significantly, Poe opens the stanza with an image (ruined) of light and modulates without transition to sound (immediately identified as "language") and its mechanically repetitive impossibility. In "The Haunted Palace," mental derangement is visually and audibly presented by means of "Vast forms that move fantastically/ To a discordant melody." (The final words of the poem are "no more.") That image much resembles the "motley drama" of "The Conqueror Worm," where Horror is "the soul of the plot." In "The Raven," the dead heroine Lenore has in fact no name at all in this world; the bird's name is "Nevermore"; and the name is an obvious fake. "Sonnet—Silence" examines such matters more fully and more mysteriously. In any case, there are two silences, "sea and shore—/ Body and Soul," and of the two the corporate silence is named "No more" and can be dealt with, while the shadow (nameless) cannot. "Commend thyself to God."

The same goes for the fiction and sketches and critical essays. In "William Wilson" (which is not his true name), the tale of a pathological young American villain ruined in an English boarding school and elsewhere, the double's voice, that is, the narrator's whisper of conscience which the narrative exists to murder, is a *"singular whisper"* and *"the very echo of my own."* As Poe says, "it was the pregnancy of solemn admonition in the singular, low,

179

hissing utterance; and, above all, it was the character, the tone, *the key*, of those few, simple, and familiar, yet *whispered* syllables [his own name], which came with a thousand thronging memories of by-gone days, and struck upon my soul with the shock of a galvanic battery." Clearly Walt Whitman took *that* story in: it is a major source for "Out of the Cradle Endlessly Rocking." In the end of Poe's narrative, the whisper becomes a full voice, but it is impossible to tell which person, which poet, which country is talking: " '*You have conquered, and I yield. Yet, henceforward art thou also dead—dead to the World, to Heaven and to Hope! In me didst thou exist—and, in my death, see by this image, which is thine own, how utterly thou hast murdered thyself.*' " In "A Descent Into the Maelström," Poe more nationalistically features an "appalling voice, half shriek, half roar, such as not even the mighty cataract of Niagara ever lifts up in its agony to Heaven." In "Silence—A Fable," in a land where " 'there is no quiet . . . nor silence,' " the Demon-protagonist espies " 'a huge gray rock' " upon which are engraved the letters " 'DESOLATION.' " Then he calls hippopotami from " 'the recesses of the morass' " nearby; they " 'roared loudly and fearfully . . . and the man [the victim of all this] trembled.' " Then the Demon " 'grew angry and cursed, with the curse of *silence*, the river, and the lilies, and the wind, and the forest, and the heaven, and the thunder, and the sighs of the water-lilies. And they became accursed, and *were still*. . . . And I looked upon the characters of the rock, and they were changed;—and the characters were SILENCE.' " The man's face " 'was wan with terror' " and " 'there was no voice throughout the vast illimitable desert.' " It is the great fable about the language of American poetry, and it reappears much later in *The Waste Land* and other desert places.

"How very commonly we hear it remarked," Poe remarked in his March 1846 *Marginalia*, "that such and such thoughts are beyond the compass of words! I do not believe that any thought, properly so called, is out of the reach of language." Then he goes on to speak of "a class of fancies [I use the word *fancies* at random, and merely because I must use *some* word], of exquisite delicacy, which are *not* thoughts, and to which, *as yet*, I have found it absolutely impossible to adapt language." The fancies sound almost like unwritten Poe poems, American poems. They constitute "a glimpse of the spirit's outer world; and I arrive at this conclusion—if this term is at all applicable to instantaneous intuition—by a perception that the delight experienced has, as its element, but *the absoluteness of novelty*. . . . It is as if the five senses were supplanted by five myriad others alien to mortality. Now, so entire is my faith in the *power of words*, that, at times, I have believed it possible to embody even the evanescence of fancies such as I have attempted to describe."

For all his horror of noise and silence, Poe's commitment to language was total, and he thereby spans the extremes of the Americans' linguistic dilemma. He worked out the positive side of the problem in "The Power of Words," a sketch in which the usual Poesque silence accedes to the secular Logos. A couple of "angels" are discussing the unbounded creativity of man. ("Speak to me," says the newly-arrived one, "in the earth's familiar tones.") Creativity is from physical motion, which is from thought, which is from God, Who, we discover toward the end of *Eureka*, is the pulse-beat of man.

> *Agathos.*—And while I thus spoke, did there not cross your mind some thought of the *physical power of words*? Is not every word an impulse on the air?
>
> *Oinos.*—But why, Agathos, do you weep?—and why—oh why do your wings droop as we hover above this fair star—which is the greenest and yet most terrible of all we have encountered in our flight? Its brilliant flowers look like a fairy dream—but its fierce volcanoes like the passions of a turbulent heart.
>
> *Agathos.*—They *are*!—they *are*! This wild star—it is now three centuries since with clasped hands, and with streaming

eyes, at the feet of my beloved—I spoke it—with a few passion-
ate sentences—into birth. Its brilliant flowers *are* the dearest of all
unfulfilled dreams, and its raging volcanoes *are* the passions of
the most turbulent and unhallowed of hearts.

Brilliant flowers and raging volcanoes at the feet of the beloved:
there in fewest, aptest words, is our gloriously tormented American
poetry, old Lucifer in harness. For two centuries—counting from
the effective beginnings of the American Revolution—our poets
have with agony, heroism, and exultation (and quite a few pas-
sionate sentences) been speaking it into birth. There was, however,
as we have seen again and again, a birth trauma. There is always
in America a trauma, a rending of medium and culture. We all of
us—poets, readers, and nonreaders—live it every day, and it is a
damned difficult game. Reversing Poe, William Carlos Williams
reminds us in *Paterson* that "it is dangerous to leave written that
which is badly written. A chance word, upon paper, may destroy
the world"; and then, consonant with the constituting metaphor of
Whitman's whole work: "Only one answer: write carelessly so that
nothing that is not green will survive."

4 July 1973   EDWIN FUSSELL

182